The Truth About The Pre-Trib Rapture

"Debunking The Devil's Lie"

Minister Andrew Hooper

Detroit MI USA

The Truth About The Pre-Trib Rapture

Andrew Hooper Publications
204300 Civic Center Dr. • Southfield, MI **48033**
Email: Andrewhooper74.ah@gmail.com
URL:

ISBN 13:   978-0-578-81973-0

ISBN 10:   0-578-81973-0

Editing by Robert Anderson and Michelle Turner

Cover, and Interior design by Robert L. Anderson

Printed in the United States of America

TABLE OF CONTENTS

ACKNOWLEDGMENTS

I, Minister Andrew Hooper, wholeheartedly acknowledge the Triune God who inspired this writing and gave me the boldness to push through so that the body of Christ would have the truth, the whole truth, and nothing but the God-inspired truth.

Without the Holy Spirit, this book would have not been possible. I thank Him for giving me this assignment and leading me line by line so that we may stand on a sure foundation.

I am also thankful for Dr. Walter Martin inspiring videos that helped me get closer to the truth.

Special thanks to following people:

Pastor Emory Moss for being a great teacher of apologetics, eschatology, and Biblical Hermeneutics. without the foundation that he helped to lay this would have not been possible for me to achieve. thanks for all the classes and push back.

Pastor Robert Anderson that one brother who is always in the fox hole with me whether in the streets, online, or in the classroom this is a brother you can depend on. I thank you for supplying a platform that has inspired me and others to constantly defend the faith that was delivered to the saints. Without your ambition and drive, I might be standing still. I commend your work ethics and drive to save lives, and patiently enduring with me as you stayed up many nights putting in endless hours of work to help me form this work for our LORD and SAVIOR. I'm sure you will hear well done my good and faithful servant. GOD bless you Brother.

Acknowledgments

INTRODUCTION

There are several reasons why I wrote this book. The first being the unction of God. I remember being in numerous classes and learning about the three different views on the Rapture. I pondered, would God have us to teach three different views as truth knowing that there is only one true view?

It always puzzled me that some teachers said that the Rapture was not an essential doctrine. Even so many brothers and sisters in the faith would regurgitate the three different views as nonessentials; but I could never get a verse and scripture that said there are nonessentials in the Word of God.

I begin to research the accuracy of the things that I had been taught about the Pre-trib Rapture; I questioned my Biblical Instructors and scholars on the various subjects of Pre-tribulation, Mid-tribulation ' and Post-tribulation.
The responses I received were superficial in nature. Their answers just did not satisfy my need to know on the subject of the Rapture and the Church. I could not drop the subject.

; Wrath

Introduction

CHAPTER ONE

WHAT IS THE ORIGIN OF THE PRI-TRIBULATION RAPTURE?

According to the overwhelming evidence that is being revealed, there appears to be a recurring pattern with known scholars that should be troubling to believers.

In the book of **Acts 17:11**, in Berea, Paul had taught the Gospel of Jesus Christ using what was written. After his sermon, those Jews who were more noble minded than others did not only eagerly receive the message in his sermon, but **they examine** what **he said daily** under the light of **Scriptures**.

> ➤ They **checked** and **verified** the accuracy of what he taught according to what was written in the Scripture.

Today, even we should use that same approach. Just because someone is more published than others, it does not make what they published Biblical even if it is related to the Biblical and in the Christian section of a Bible bookstore. We should verify the information anyone gives us as coming from the Word of GOD. Whether in book form or on Sunday mornings.

It seems that in these latter-days that many in the Church has turned away from that practice and have started to observe how '**many letters**' a man has behind his name or how many books he has published. In **1st Corinthians 1:27** "But God has chosen the foolish things of the world to put to shame the wise...."
Isn't it time that we get back to the basics and search things daily to find out if they are truly the things that Christ taught?

According to Dr. Walter Martin, "The Christian Church believed for nineteen centuries [*the church fathers, the reformers, every great theologian in the entire history of the church*] up until the last one hundred and forty years believed

- we would see the anti-Christ and
- that we would be persecuted by him and
- that we would be delivered from him by the second coming of Jesus Christ.

The ideal that we are going to escape the anti-Christ does not surface until approximately one hundred and forty years ago when a fifteen-year-old girl, is said to, had a revelation. And that revelation was pickup by **John Nelson Darby** [mid-

1800s] the founder of the Plymouth Brethren. It developed into a form of theology known as the **Dispensational Theology**."[1]

HISTORICAL DEVELOPMENT OF THE PRE-TRIB RAPTURE:

Paul N. Benware, in his book, Understanding End Times Prophecy, notes that many writers in the 17th and 18th Centuries began to speak of **a Rapture separate and apart from the Second Coming**:[2]

".....several citations demonstrate that an imminent return of Christ prior to the second coming was believed in by others long before Darby. [3]
- As early as 1687, Peter Jurieu, in his book Approaching Deliverance of the Church (1687), taught that Christ would come in the air to rapture the saints and return to heaven before the battle of Armageddon. He spoke of a secret rapture prior to His coming in glory and judgment at Armageddon.[4]
- About fifty years later, Philip Doddridge's commentary on the New Testament (1738) and John Gill's commentary on the New Testament (1748) both used the term rapture and speak of it as imminent.

It is clear that these men believed that *this coming* will precede Christ's descent to the earth and the time of judgment. The purpose was to preserve believers from the time of judgment.
James Macknight (1763) and Thomas Scott (1792) taught that the righteous will be carried into heaven, where they will be secure until the time of judgment is over. [5]

Although a detailed chronology is not given by these writers, it is evident that they did see a distinction between the rapture and the second coming and saw the rapture as preceding the time of judgment. Why did these and other writers begin to speak of a rapture that was distinct from the second coming and see believers removed from the earth prior to the judgments? The answer is that once a literal approach to interpreting the Scriptures began to be rediscovered, these truths started to emerge."

"This is not to say, of course, that up until the last century no one in the church had ideas about eschatology. But a precise formulation of eschatology has been a recent development, and this would include views within all the rapture positions. It is, therefore, less than fair or accurate to say that pre-tribulationism ought to be set aside because it is a recent doctrinal formulation. Having said this, however, it must be observed that

[1] https://www.youtube.com/watch?v=SA_rEAX0aeE Dr. Walter Martin (May 22, 2020
[2] Benware, Paul. Understanding End Times Prophecy: A Comprehensive Approach . Moody Publishers. Kindle Edition.
[3] Grant R. Jeffrey, Apocalypse (Toronto: Frontier Research, 1992), 313-22.
[4] Grant R. Jeffrey, "Was the PreTrib Position of the Rapture Seen Before John Darby?" 2-3. A paper presented to the PretribStudy Group, 15 December 1993, Dallas, Texas.
[5] Ibid 3-9

J. N. Darby did not originate the idea that the rapture and the second coming were two distinct events and that the rapture removed the church from the tribulation period."[6]

As early as the 1740's Morgan Edwards was espousing a pre-tribulational viewpoint in his writings about eschatology. The difference in his view and the modern Pre-Trib concept is that he believed the Rapture would occur in the middle of Daniel's 70th week, about 3 1/2 years before the Second Coming.[7]

THE MODERN PRE-TRIB VIEW:

The person who crystallized the modern Pre-Trib viewpoint was a man named John Darby (1800-1882).[8] Darby was born in London and was trained in the law. He practiced law for only one year before he was overcome by a deep spiritual struggle that finally led to a decision to enter the ministry. He became an Anglican priest but quickly became disillusioned when the church decreed that all converts would have to swear allegiance to the King of England. Darby considered this to be a compromise with the lordship of Christ.

Darby decided to leave the Anglican Church. In the years following, he and other dissenters from the established state church inaugurated a movement that came to be known as **the Plymouth Brethren**.

In 1826 Darby broke one of his legs, and during the long convalescence that followed, he engaged in an intensive study of the Scriptures that convinced him of the clear distinction between the Church and Israel. He also became convicted of the imminent return of Jesus.
- Thus, by 1827 he had developed the fundamental principles that would come to characterize a new theological system that would be called **Dispensationalism**.
- After John Darby refined the concept, **it spread rapidly** throughout Europe and America.

The viewpoint has always been blessed by gifted communicators.[9]
- In 1878 the very first best-selling prophecy book incorporated the idea. It was Jesus is Coming by William E. Blackstone (1841-1935).[10]
- In 1909 the very first study Bible ever published — The Scofield Study Bible — developed the scriptural arguments for the viewpoint in detail. Scofield incorporated **Darby's Pre-tri Rapture** into his Scofield Reference Bible[11]
- Then came the amazing charts and diagrams of Clarence Larkin (1850-1924) in his book Dispensational Truth.[12]

[6] Benware, Paul. Understanding End Times Prophecy: A Comprehensive Approach . Moody Publishers. Kindle Edition.
[7] Tommy Ice, "Morgan Edwards: A Pre-Darby Rapturist," The Conservative Theological Journal, April 1997, pages 4-12.
[8] Tim LaHaye, "Target Number One," Pre-Trib Perspectives, September 2002, pages 1-3.
[9] https://christinprophecy.org/articles/the-origin-of-the-concept-of-a-pre-tribulation-rapture/ (May 22, 2020)
[10] William E. Blackstone, Jesus is Coming (1878). The modern day version is published by Kregel (1989).
[11] C. I. Scofield, The Scofield Study Bible (London: Oxford University Press, 1909).
[12] Clarence Larkin, Dispensational Truth (Philadelphia, 1920)

- Harry Ironside (1876-1951), the popular pastor of the Moody Memorial Church in Chicago, preached the concept in his sermons and books during the 1930's and 40's.[13]
- In 1970 Hal Lindsey published The Late Great Planet Earth and once again the viewpoint was expressed in a best seller.[14]

The 20th Century ended with the view being espoused in the "Left Behind" block-buster series of books written by Tim LaHaye and Jerry Jenkins.[15]

ANCIENT EXAMPLES OF THE CONCEPT:

Quite significant is the fact that more than a thousand years before Darby the writings of one known as "**Pseudo-Ephraem**" (4th-7th century AD) spoke of the saints being removed from the earth and taken to be with the Lord prior to the judgments of the tribulation. He taught that there were two distinct comings and that the church was removed before the tribulation.[16]

Thomas D. Ice, The Rapture in Pseudo-Ephraem's Rapture Statement:[17]
"I vividly remember the phone call at my office late one afternoon from Canadian prophecy teacher and writer Grant Jeffrey.[18] He told me that he had found an **ancient pre-trib rapture statement**. I said, "Let's hear it." He read the following to me over the phone:

All the saints and elect of God are gathered together before the tribulation, which is to come, and are taken to the Lord, in order that they may not see at any time the confusion which overwhelms the world because of our sins.

I said that it sure sounds like a pre-trib statement and began to fire at him all the questions I have since received many times when telling others about the statement from **Pseudo-Ephraem's sermon On the Last Times, the Antichrist, and the End of the World**.""[19]

One of the early Church Fathers, **The Shepherd of Hermas**, writing in the early 2nd Century, makes an interesting observation about "the great tribulation that is coming." He says,

*"If then ye prepare yourselves, and repent with all your heart and turn to the Lord, it will be possible **for you to escape it**, if your heart be pure and spotless, and ye spend the rest of the days of your life in serving the Lord blamelessly."*[20]

---

[13] Ed Reese, "Henry (Harry) Allan Ironside"
[14] Hal Lindsey with C. C. Carlson, The Late Great Planet Earth (Grand Rapids, MI: Zondervan, 1970).
[15] Beginning in 1996 Tim LaHaye and Jerry Jenkins started publishing a series of scriptural novels about the Rapture which came to be known as "The Left Behind" books. A total of 12 volumes have been published in the series, and to date, they have sold 55 million copies.
[16] Ibid.
[17] Timothy Demy and Thomas Ice, "The Rapture and Pseudo-Ephraem: An Early Medieval Citation," Bibliotheca Sacra 152 (July-September 1995): 1-13.
[18] For more information on the Pseudo-Ephraem statement see Grant R. Jeffrey, Final Warning (Toronto: Frontier Research Publications, 1995). Forthcoming, Timothy Demy and Thomas Ice, "The Rapture and an Early Medieval Citation" Bibliotheca Sacra 152 (July 1995): 300-11. Grant R. Jeffrey, "A Pretribulational Rapture Statement in the Early Medieval Church" in Thomas Ice and Timothy Demy, ed., When the Trumpet Sounds: Today's Foremost Authorities Speak Out on End-Time Controversies (Eugene, Or: Harvest House, 1995).
[19] Grant Jeffrey found the statement in Paul J. Alexander, The Byzantine Apocalyptic Tradition, by (Berkeley: University of California Press, 1985), 2.10. The late Alexander found the sermon in C. P. Caspari, ed. Briefe, Abhandlungen und Predigten aus den zwei letzten Jahrhunderten des kirchlichen Altertums und dem Anfang des Mittelaters, (Christiania, 1890), 208-20. This German work also contains Caspari's commentary on the sermon on pages 429-72.
[20] The Shepherd of Hermas, 2[23]:5. A copy of the complete writings of The Shepherd of Hermas can be found on the Internet.

Note: But The copies of **The Shepherd of Hermas** that I have does not validate that claim, unless you read into it what is NOT there:

> '*Stand steadfast, you who work righteousness, and do not doubt, so that your journey may be with the holy angels. Happy are you who endure the **great tribulation** that is coming on, and happy are those who will not hold back their own life.*'[21]

> '"*You escaped from it well," she said, "because you cast your care on God and opened your heart to the Lord, believing that you can be saved by none other than His great and glorious name. Because of this the Lord sent His angel Thegri, who has rule over the beasts, and shut its mouth so that it cannot tear you. You have escaped from **great tribulation** because of your faith, and because you did not doubt in the presence of such a beast. Therefore go and tell the elect of the Lord His mighty deeds, and say to them that this beast is a type of the **great tribulation** that is coming.*'

PRE-TRIBULATION RAPTURE VIEW

Statement of view – Christ will come for his saints; afterward, he will come with his saints. The first stage of Christ's coming is called the rapture; the second is called the Revelation. One of the main focuses is whether the church experiences the wrath of God and goes through the tribulation period to the end. Or are they raptured out before the tribulation starts unto safety.

---

[21] Ibid p. 16

CHAPTER TWO

WHAT DID JESUS TEACH ABOUT RESCUING THE CHURCH?

Did Jesus teach that He would be back to rescue the Church before the Great Tribulation?

As we begin to examine the evidence, let's look at a passage to determine if what certain writers have been promoting is truthful in comparison to what the Scriptures provide as the infallible word of GOD. As students of the Word of God, we should always do a side by side comparison to confirm the information provided. If the information cannot be validated, we should reject what man has written. The passage below is from The Moody Handbook of Theology. Let's see if what was provided about John chapter 14:1-3 is a valid analysis.

> *"**The rapture**.* Although John does not provide an explicit statement concerning the rapture as does Paul, *John undoubtedly refers to the rapture in John 14:1-3. The rapture is related to the church, and Jesus was speaking to the nucleus of disciples that would compose the small beginnings of the church in Acts 2.*
> Because the disciples were grieving at the imminent departure of Christ in John 14, He encouraged them by reminding them (as the infant church) that He was going to prepare dwelling places for them in His Father's home. His promise to return and take them to Himself self (John 14:3) is understood as parallel to Paul's statement in 1 Thessalonians 4:13-18."[22]

Let us examine one of the most *controversial text* that people use to try and prove this:

> *"Don't let your heart be troubled. Believe in God; believe also in me. 2 In my Father's house are many rooms; if not, I would have told you. I am going away to prepare a place for you. 3 If I go away and prepare a place for you, I will come again and take you to myself, so that where I am you may be also."* **John 14:1-3 (CSB)**

In verses 1-3 the claim is that Jesus has went to prepare a place for the church, and that he is coming back to receive the church unto Himself before the Great Tribulation.

---

[22] Paul Enns. The Moody Handbook of Theology (Kindle Locations 1401-1405). Kindle Edition.

Now the premise is true about Him coming back to receive the Church as a whole.

The problem arises when certain teachers start to Insert and to teach that CHRIST would return at a time the word of God does not affirm. Giving false narratives that Christ did not teach or say, is called eisegesis; Reading information into the text that is not provided from the text. Henceforth, the view that we will be addressing is **the pre-tribulation rapture of the Church**.

CONCERNS: DISCIPLES AND JESUS – JOHN 13-14:

"'Lord," Simon Peter said to him, "where are you going? Jesus answered, "Where I am going you cannot follow me now, but you will follow later." 37 "Lord," Peter asked, "why can't I follow you now? I will lay down my life for you." 38 Jesus replied, "Will you lay down your life for me? Truly I tell you, a rooster will not crow until you have denied me three times.' **John 13:36-38(CSB)**

"Don't let your heart be troubled. Believe in God; believe also in me. 2 In my Father's house are many rooms; if not, I would have told you. I am going away to prepare a place for you. 3 If I go away and prepare a place for you, I will come again and take you to myself, so that where I am you may be also. 4 You know the way to where I am going." 5 "Lord," Thomas said, "we don't know where you're going. How can we know the way?" 6 Jesus told him, "I am the way, the truth, and the life. No one comes to the Father except through me. 7 If you know me, you will also know my Father. From now on you do know him and have seen him."' **John 14:1-7 (CSB)**

John 14:1-3 is the answer to what Simon Peter asked in John chapter **13:36**:

- **Simon Peter said** unto him, Lord, **whither goes thou?**
  - ○ **Jesus answered him**, *Whither I go,*
    - ➤ *thou canst follow me now;*
    - ➤ *but thou shalt follow me afterwards.*
- **Peter said unto him**, Lord, **why cannot *I* follow thee now?** *I* will lay down my life for thy sake.
  - ○ **Jesus Replied:** *Don't let your heart be troubled. Believe in God; believe also in me. 2 In my Father's house are many rooms; if not, I would have told you.*
    - ➤ ***I am going away to prepare a place for you. 3 If I go away and prepare a place for you,***
    - ➤ ***I will come again and take you to myself, so that where I am you may be also.***

In the original text there was no chapter breaks, And the reader had to follow, the natural flow of the conversation. **Jesus was not** telling Peter that he was **coming back** to **rescue the church before the Great Tribulation**, He was telling him that he was preparing The Kingdom of GOD for the arrival of all believers who would be alive and be resurrected at HIS second coming.

> *"And He will set the sheep on His right hand, but the goats on the left. 34 Then the King will say to those on His right hand, 'Come, you blessed of My Father, **inherit the kingdom prepared for you from the foundation of the world:**"* **Matthew 25:33-34 (NKJV)**

Furthermore, Peter would have understood the **return of Christ** in the same manner as did Martha:

> *"No one can come to me unless the Father who sent me draws him, and **I will raise him up on the last day**."* **John 6:44 (CSB)**

> *"Martha said to him, "I know that he will rise **again in the resurrection at the last day**."* **John 11:24 (CSB)**

Christ would return at the end of the age in the last day when the resurrection happens. Peter also taught the same message that he received from Christ:

> *While they were speaking to the people, the priests, the captain of the temple police, and the Sadducees confronted them, 2 because they were annoyed that they were teaching the people and proclaiming in Jesus the resurrection of the dead.* **Acts 4:1-2 (CSB)**

Just as Peter had questioned the Lord about where He was going, Thomas also did not understand that Jesus was talking about returning to heaven from where He had come. In context of the questions and Jesus response to His Disciples, there is no possible way for pre-tribulationist to use these passages to support their false premise of a pre-tribulation rapture:

- **Jesus says,** "And whither I go ye know, and the way ye know. "(verse 4)
  - ○ **"Thomas saith** unto him, Lord, we know not whither thou goest; and how can we know the way?" (verse 5)
- **"Jesus saith** unto him,
  - ➢ I **am the way**, the **truth**, and the **life**:
  - ➢ no man **cometh unto the Father**, but by me. "(verse 6)

Notice the context of the conversation it is not a **rescue,** but the promise of **entering the Kingdom of GOD**. For all those who would seek **eternal life**, Jesus is saying, the **truth** is **I am** the **only way** to the **Father**. Preparation is through the cross: His Death, Burial, Resurrection, and Ascension.

Our understanding of John chapter 14 should not be that this is a **rescue** of GOD'S people or a **rapture of the Church**, but exactly what Jesus was conveying to His disciples that He was going to make preparations for believers who followed Him in the manner of obedience and faith.

Read the whole chapter 14:1-31. This is the true context.

Probing the collective information of all the parables in Jesus teachings, starting with Luke chapter 21, we'll look at the time frame He gives in the accounts of His life, death, burial, resurrection, and return. And we will also highlight the information that others have read into the text.

DID JESUS TEACH A PRE-TRIBULATION RAPTURE? CONCERNS: DISCIPLES AND JESUS - LUKE 21:

> "*These things that you see — the days will come when not one stone will be left on another that will not be thrown down.*" 7 "**Teacher,**" **they asked him,**
> - ✔ "*so when will these things happen?*
> - ✔ *And what will be the sign when these things are about to take place?*"

> *Note: Matthew says:*
> 1. "*Tell us, when will **these things happen?***
> 2. *And what is **the sign of your coming***
> 3. *and **of the end of the age?**" **24:3 (CSB)***

> 8 Then he said, "**Watch out** *that you are not deceived.*
> - *For **many will come** in my name, saying, '**I am he,**' and, '**The time is near.**' Don't follow them.* 9
> - *When you hear of wars and rebellions, don't be alarmed. Indeed, it is necessary that these things take place first, but **the end won't come right away.**"*

Note: There is no mention of a pre-tribulation rapture in verses 10-12.

> 10 Then he told them:
> - "*Nation will be raised up against nation, and kingdom against kingdom.* 11

- *There will be violent earthquakes, and famines and plagues in various places, and there will be terrifying sights and great signs from heaven.*

12 But before all these things,

- **they will lay their hands on you** and **persecute you**.
- *They will hand you over to the synagogues and prisons,*
- *and you will be brought before kings and governors because of my name. 13* **This will give you an opportunity to bear witness**.

14 Therefore make up your minds not to prepare your defense ahead of time, 15 for I will give you such words and a wisdom that none of your adversaries will be able to resist or contradict. 16 You will even be betrayed by parents, brothers, relatives, and friends.

- **They will kill some of you.** *17*
- *You will be hated by everyone because of my name, 18* **but not a hair of your head will be lost**.

19 **By your endurance**, gain your lives. 20 **"When you see Jerusalem surrounded by armies,**

- *then recognize that its desolation has come near. 21*
- *Then those in Judea must flee to the mountains.*
- *Those inside the city must leave it, and those who are in the country must not enter it, 22*

because these are days of vengeance to fulfill all the things that are written. 23 Woe to pregnant women and nursing mothers in those days,

Note: There is no mention of a pre-tribulation rapture in verses 24-28.

- for there will be great distress in the land and wrath against this people. 24
- **They will be killed by the sword** and be led captive into all the nations,

and Jerusalem will be trampled by the Gentiles **until the times of the Gentiles are fulfilled.** 25

- *"Then there will be signs in the sun, moon, and stars; and there will be anguish on the earth among nations bewildered by the roaring of the sea and the waves. 26* **People will faint from fear and expectation of the things that are coming on the world,** *because the powers of the heavens will be shaken. 27*
- *Then* **they will see the Son of Man coming in a cloud** *with power and great glory.*

28 But when these things begin to take place, stand up and lift up your heads, because **your redemption is near.**" **Luke 21:6-28(CSB)**

Notice in verse 28 Jesus says:

1. "to stand up"
2. "lift Up your heads"
3. "your redemption is near."

These instructions are given to believers. It is not addressed to Israel but to the disciples, which in turn is applied to all followers of Christ who will be watching for His return. As the passage continues Jesus gives His followers the parable of the fig tree which is about *times and seasons*. At verse 31 He says:

> "*In the same way, when you see these things happening, recognize that the kingdom of God is near.*" **Luke 21:31 (CSB)**

Note: The Times of the Gentiles clarified: It is a reference of the Jews being under **Gentile Control**. The time of Gentile dominion ends with **the return of Christ**. In **Revelation 11:2**, John indicates that Jerusalem will be under **Gentile rule**, even though the temple has been restored. The armies of the Beast are destroyed by the Lord in **Revelation 19:17–19**, just before the millennial reign of Christ is initiated. When the time is right, God will restore the entire Nation of Israel, and they will come to faith in Him, through Jesus Christ, once again, ending "the times of the Gentiles (**rule**)" (Isaiah 17:7; 62:11–12; Romans 11:26).[23]

Carefully exegeting *Luke Chapter 21*, above, we note:
1) Jesus both addressed and explained to his disciples their two pressing questions (*7*). He gives them prophetic information of **what shall** and **must come to pass**.
2) Jesus is **privately** (Matt. 24:3) addressing His disciples (His followers/believers), Jews.
3) Jesus warns His followers not to be deceived (*8*).
4) This was not a message to the **Nation of Israel**, even though it concerned Israel (*5, 20-24*). The Nation had rejected Jesus and was [is] in Apostasy (Matt 23:37-39). They were not listening.
5) Jesus message addressed what would happen among all nations, not just Israel (*10,25-26*).

---

6) Jesus says, but before all these things happen, they shall persecute **the disciples of that time** (*12*).
7) It is His followers; the disciples are the YOU who other **Jews and gentiles** would lay hands on and persecute because of His Name (*12*).
8) The **Nation of Israel** and **non-believing gentiles** would be His followers' adversaries and kill some of them because of His Name (*16-17*).
9) However, notice, there is never any mention of the miraculous **pre-tribulation rapture** in any of His messages.
10) Jesus reveals the events that did not happen during **the disciples' life span** (*24-25*). Such as
   - **The times of the Gentile being fulfilled.**
   - **The signs from heaven** and the great signs which will happen later we see this in the book of **Revelation 6:12-15. Please read.**

When read in context of the events, there is no mention of the rapture taking place.

Is the Church to believe that Jesus left out this **significant event** in His message because it is a mystery, and He does not want us to know when the rapture will take place?

I **DON'T THINK SO, WE SHALL FIND OUT**.

ISRAEL AND THE CHURCH

Contrary to those who contend that the passages in Luke 21:13-28 addressed the time period for Israel only and that the church has already been raptured, I would suggest they read the book of **Revelation chapter 12:12-17.**

Since we know the book of revelation uses symbols, we need to determine who is **the woman** that the serpent makes war with and where do we get that symbol from?

Beginning with Jacob's son, Joseph's, vision:

> "And he dreamed yet another dream, and told it his brethren, and said, Behold, I have dreamed a dream more; and, behold,
>   - *the sun*
>   - *and the moon*
>   - *and the eleven stars*

> *made obeisance to me. 10 And he told it to his father, and to his brethren: and his father rebuked him, and said unto him, What is this dream that thou hast dreamed? Shall I and thy mother and thy brethren indeed come to bow down ourselves to thee to the earth? 11 And his brethren envied him; but his father observed the saying.* **Genesis 37:9-11(KJV)**

Jacob did not have any trouble identifying the symbolic meaning of the **sun, moon, and stars** - "Shall **I** and **your** mother and **your** brothers bow down to you?"
- The sun represented the father,
- The moon the mother,
- The stars the sons (Joseph's eleven brothers).

UNDERSTANDING THE CONTEXT - REVELATION CHAPTER 12:

> "*And there appeared a great wonder in heaven;*
> - *a woman clothed with the sun, and the moon under her feet,*
> - *and upon her head a crown of twelve stars: 2*
> - *And she being with child cried, travailing in birth, and pained to be delivered.*" **Revelation 12:1-2 (KJV)**

❖ **The Woman is Israel. Note:** This woman is **not** the Church.

❖ **The Twelve Stars are the twelve tribes of Israel. Note:** The Church is **Not** Israel, and the **Church** does **Not** replace Israel.

❖ **Child is the Messiah (Jesus Christ). Note:** It is **Not** the Church that births the Messiah.

> "*And his tail drew the third part of the stars of heaven, and did cast them to the earth: and the dragon stood before*
> - *the woman which was ready to be delivered,*
> *for to devour*
> - *her child as soon as it was born. 5*
> - *And she brought forth a man child, who was to rule all nations with a rod of iron:*
> - *and her child was caught up unto God, and to his throne.* **Revelation 12:4-5 (KJV)**

While it is true that Mary gave birth to Jesus, it is also true that **Jesus, the son of David from the tribe of Judah, came from Israel**. In a sense, Israel gave birth—or brought forth—Christ Jesus.[24]

---

[24] https://www.gotquestions.org/Revelation-chapter-12.html (May 22, 2020)

Verse 5 is illustrative of Jesus who ascended to heaven (Acts 1:9-11) and will one day establish His kingdom on earth (Revelation 20:4-6), and He will rule it with perfect judgment (the "rod of iron"; see Psalm 2:7-9).

*"**Therefore** rejoice, ye heavens, and ye that dwell in them. Woe to the inhabiters of the earth and of the sea! for the devil is come down unto you, **having great wrath**, because **he knoweth that he hath but a short time**. 13 And when the dragon saw that he was cast unto the earth,*
- *he persecuted **the woman which brought forth the man child**. 14*

*And to the woman were given two wings of a great eagle, that she might fly into the wilderness, into her place, where she is nourished for **a time, and times, and half a time**, from the face of the serpent. 15*
- *And the serpent cast out of his mouth water as a **flood after the woman**, that he might cause her to be carried away of the flood.*

*16 And **the earth helped the woman**, and the earth opened her mouth, and swallowed up the flood which the dragon cast out of his mouth.*

*17 And the **dragon** was wroth with **the woman**,*
- *and went to **make war** with **the remnant of her seed**, which*
  - ➤ ***keep the commandments of God,***
  - ➤ ***and have the testimony of Jesus Christ***. "**Revelation 12:12-17(KJV)**

WHO IS THE SEED THAT THE SERPENT MAKES WAR WITH?

Therefore, the symbolic language in verse 17 is figurative of two groups (**Israel** and the **Church [Jews** and **Gentiles]**). Both groups are connected to the Jewish Messiah. In Context of the complete Scriptures, it is impractical to say the Dragon makes war on one group, and not the other. We see the evidence provided by scripture and conclude that both groups are going through this event just as the word of GOD has determined.

It is Not just the Nation of Israel who is persecuted, but the Church of Jesus Christ. The source of all true persecution is Satan, and his target is God. Satan not only hates God, but he also hates all who bear His holy image in them by means of His Spirit. He hates those who has the testimony of Jesus Christ; Keep in mind what Jesus taught his followers in **Luke 21:12, 16-19**.

> "*In fact, all who want to live a godly life in Christ Jesus will* **be persecuted**." **2 Timothy 3:12 (CSB)**

WHO DOES THE BIBLE SAY IS THE SEED?

"*Now to Abraham and his seed were the promises made. He saith* **not**, *And to seeds, as of many;*
- **but as of one**,
- *And to thy seed,* **which is Christ**." **Galatians 3:16 (KJV)**

"*For* **ye are all the children of God**
- **by faith** *in Christ Jesus. 27*
- *For* **as many of you** *as have been baptized* **into Christ** *have* **put on Christ**." **Galatians 3:26-27 (KJV)**

"*There is neither* **Jew** *nor* **Greek**, *there is neither bond nor free, there is neither male nor female:*
- *for* **ye are all one** *in Christ Jesus. 29*
- *And if ye be Christ's,*
  - ➤ *then are ye* **Abraham's seed**,
  - ➤ *and* **heirs according to the promise**." **Galatians 3:28-29 (KJV)**

'*Jesus replied, "Truly I tell you, unless someone is* **born again**,
- *he cannot see the kingdom of God."*' **John 3:3 (CSB)**

"*Blessed be the God and Father of our Lord Jesus Christ. Because of his great mercy*
- *he has given* **us new birth** *into a living hope*
- **through the resurrection of Jesus** *Christ from the dead*." **1 Peter 1:3 (CSB)**

"*He predestined* **us to be adopted as sons**
- *through* **Jesus Christ** *for himself,*
- *according to the good pleasure of his will,*" **Ephesians 1:5 (CSB)**

"*You did not receive a spirit of slavery to fall back into fear. Instead, you received* **the Spirit of adoption**, *by whom we cry out, "Abba, Father!" 16*
- *The Spirit himself testifies together with our spirit that* **we are God's children**, *17 and if children,*
- *also heirs* — **heirs of God and coheirs with Christ** — *if indeed we suffer with him so that we may also be glorified with him. Romans 8:15-17 (CSB)*

In conclusion, there is no way that anyone could deny that the seed that Satan goes to make war with is the body of Christ who keeps the commandments of God and have the testimony of Christ.

The Parable of The Faithful Steward – Luke 12:41-46:

Notice in context of the verse, Peter verifies that the parable is addressed to **all servants of the Lord**.

> "Then **Peter said** unto him, Lord, speakest thou this parable unto us, or **even to all**?" **Luke 12:41 (KJV)**

Jesus expresses the reward which will be given to all those faithful servants at His return, which is rulership with Him,

> "And the Lord said, Who then is that faithful and wise steward, whom his lord shall **make ruler over his household,** to give them their portion of meat in due season? 43
> - **Blessed is that servant,** whom his lord when he cometh shall find so doing. 44
>   - Of a truth I say unto you, **that he will make him ruler over all that he hath**." **Luke 12:42-44 (KJV)**

Contrary to those who contend that the passages are just for a Jewish audience, Scripture proves that it also applies to the church:

> Behold, I stand at the door, and knock: if any man hear my voice, and open the door,
> - I will come in to him, and will sup with him, and he with me. 21 To him that overcometh
>   - will I grant **to sit with me in my throne,** even as I also overcame, and am set down with my Father in his throne. 22
>   - He that hath an ear, let him hear **what the Spirit saith unto the churches**. **Revelation 3:20-22 (KJV)**

It is clear when the reader allows Scripture to interpret Scripture that the passages apply to **both groups.** There is no separation and no pre-tribulation rapture of the Church or The Nation of Israel.

> "But and if that servant say in his heart, My lord delayeth his coming; and shall begin to beat the menservants and maidens,

> and to eat and drink, and to be drunken; 46 *The lord of that* **servant** *will come in a day when he looketh not for him, and at an hour when he is not aware, and will cut him in sunder, and* **will appoint him his portion with the unbelievers***."* **Luke 12:45-46 (KJV)**

GROUP CLASSIFICATIONS

There are at least three group classifications that can be identified in Scripture:
1. The Nation of Israel (Jews and Israelites).
    a. All Jews were ethnically Israelites.
    b. All Israelites were Not ethnically Jews (Judah).
    c. This does not account for converts to the nation.
    d. The Nation of Israel is in Apostasy - **Matthew 23:37-39.**
2. Non-believers (Israelites and gentiles)
3. **The Church** (Israelites (**Jews**) and Gentiles) [*Matthew 16-18, Ephesians 2:19-20, 1 Corinthians 3:11; Acts 2:36-47; Acts 14: 27; Ephesians 3:4-7; Galatians 3:28]*:
    a. The Loveless Church - *Revelation 2:1-7.*
    b. The Compromising Church - *Revelation 2:12-17.*
    c. The Corrupt Church - *Revelation 2:18-29.*
    d. The Dead Church - *Revelation 3:1-6.*
    e. The Lukewarm Church - *Revelation 3:14-22.*
    f. **The Faithful Church** - *Revelation 3:7-13.*
    g. **The Persecuted Church** - *Revelation 2:8-11.*
    - The church is admonished to be **faithful** even unto death (2:10). In each of these, Jesus says to the Church, "I know your works" (2:2, 9, 13, 19; 3:1, 8, 15).
    - Jesus admonishes the Church to **hear** and **overcome** (2:7, 11, 17, 26, 29; 3: 5-6, 12-13, 21-22).

THE TWO MAJOR GROUPS:

Almost anyone who studies the Bible with Biblical integrity, and who is aware of world events as related to Israel and Jerusalem would acknowledge:
1. Jesus was sent to the Nation of Israel (Jews), **first**.
2. **Currently**, the Nation of Israel is in a state of apostasy because the nation rejected their Messiah.

3. **The Nation of Israel (Jews)** sacrificed their Messiah by handing Him over to the **Gentiles** (Romans) who Crucified Him.
4. Even so, Jesus built **His Church** starting with individual **believing Jews** and bringing in individual **believing Gentiles.**
5. All believers fall into the One Group **(A), the Church.**
6. All non-believers **(Nation of Israel** and **Gentiles) fall into the other Group (B).**

However, the theme of Genesis has never wavered from God's sovereign plan to reconcile **MAN** back to Himself, long before He formed Israel to be His servants in the earth.

It was sin that brought about these two groups (**Nation of Israel** and **Gentiles**). And it is Jesus that will make the two, one new MAN in Himself (Ephesians 2:15-16, 3:4-6).

The passages of 1st **Thessalonians 5:1-9**** are also addressed to the **church,** on earth. The time frame is the same as in **Luke12:41-43** (above). These believers are addressed in this same manner "**to watch;**" if they are on the earth, at the **second advent of CHRIST**.

Peter verifies that Jesus Addressed his message to all would be **servants** of the Lord (**Luke 12:41**).
- It is those **servants** who are **faithful** and **wise stewards** (**12:43**).
- It is those **servants** who are to hear and obey what the Spirit says to the **Churches** (**Revelation 3:22**) and if they hear and overcome (**3:22**), they will be granted to sit with Christ on His throne.
- It is the **servants of Christ** (the Church) that are the **Children of the light** and **children of the day** (**1st Thessalonians 5:5,8**).
- It is the **servants of Christ** who **are not appointed** to God's wrath (**5:9**) and who are to be **sober** and **watching**.

As exegeted from the text, the Church (**Jews** and **Gentiles**) are **servants** of GOD.

The **Nation of Israel is** currently an **Apostate Servant** in denial of **Jesus Christ their Messiah**, the Man and His Works (*John 19:15, Matthew 27:25*).

They along with other non-believing gentiles, who do not repent:
- belong to the night or darkness (*1ˢᵗ Thessalonians 5:4-5*).
- will not escape sudden destruction (*5:3*).
- Sleeps at night and gets drunk at night; (*5:7*).
- are appointed and will not escape God's wrath (*5:9*).

They did not watch because they did not believe.

But *the* watchful and sober *Church,* these faithful servants, will not be *overtaken by darkness* and *the day of wrath* because they are "children of the day" and "children of light" not because **they were moved out of the way** but they **consistently watched without being moved out of the way**. Also, this day does not overcome them, **but they are there to watch** for that day as it approaches.

THE PARABLE OF THE TEN MINAS:

As we exegete the parable of the Minas, note the details in Christ's teaching.

The comparison was of Himself as the nobleman going into the far country, of course, this would be His ascending into heaven. Furthermore, He points out in the parable that He is going to receive a kingdom and return. Notice how precise and straight to the point the message is.

As the nobleman in the parable He gives instruction to His servants; please note that He collects them after He returns from purchasing the kingdom that he went to receive.

When does Christ return with the kingdom? It is after the tribulation, and His message is clear.

In this parable we also see eschatology, or end time language which describes *the Kingdom of GOD returning with CHRIST* and *judgment* on those apostate servants who did not invest that which was given to them.

*"Now as they heard these things, He spoke another parable, **because** He was near Jerusalem and **because***

- *they thought **the kingdom of God would appear immediately.** 12*

*Therefore He said: "A certain nobleman went into **a far country***

- ***to receive for himself a kingdom** and to **return.** 13*

*So he called ten of his servants, delivered to them ten minas, and said to them, '**Do business till I come.'***

14 But his citizens hated him, and sent a delegation after him, saying,

- *'**We will not have this man to reign over us.'***

*15 "And so it was that when **he returned,***

- ***having received the kingdom,***

*he then commanded these servants, to whom he had given the money, to be called to him, that he might know how much every man had gained by trading. 16 Then came the first, saying, 'Master, your mina has earned ten minas.' 17 **And he said to him,***

- ***Well done, good servant;** because **you were faithful** in a very little, have authority over ten cities.'*

*18 And the second came, saying, 'Master, your mina has earned five minas.' 19 **Likewise he said to him,** 'You also be over five cities.'*

*20 "Then another came, saying, 'Master, here is your mina, which I have kept put away in a handkerchief. 21 For I feared you, because you are an austere man. You collect what you did not deposit, and reap what you did not sow.' 22 **And he said to him,***

- ***Out of your own mouth I will judge you, you wicked servant.***

*You knew that I was an austere man, collecting what I did not deposit and reaping what I did not sow. 23 Why then did you not put my money in the bank, that **at my coming** I might have **collected it with interest?'** 24 "And he said to those who stood by, 'Take the mina from him, and give it to him who has ten minas.' 25 (But they said to him, 'Master, he has ten minas.') 26 'For I say to you, that to everyone who has will be given; and from him who does not have, even what he has will be taken away from him. 27 But bring here those enemies of mine,*

- *who did not want me to reign over them, and slay them before me.'"* **Luke 19:11-27 (NKJV)**

This is another example of both groups:

- The Nation of Israel (**Jews**) who did not want **Jesus their Messiah** to reign over them (**14,22**).
- The Church (**Jews** and **Gentiles**). The good and faithful servant (**17**).

Both are being addressed with the same message: keep working unto the **return of the Christ.**

THE PARABLE OF THE WHEAT AND TARES:

Jesus paints the picture of the kingdom of heaven and compares it to a farmer's field where he has planted all His good crop. And over a period of time, while men slept an enemy came and corrupted the crop.

The main point that is being made during the time of growth the farmer would not pull out the bad seed if he did, he would uproot the good crop with it. His instructions to his servants were to let both grow together until the harvest when all things would be ready to harvest.

These parables are still very valid today as a teaching tool especially when dealing with eschatology and end times and as related to what Jesus said and taught.

"'Another parable He put forth to them, saying: **"The kingdom of heaven** is like a man who **sowed**
  • **good seed in his field**;
    25 *but while men slept, his enemy came and **sowed***
  • **tares** among the wheat and went his way.
    26 But when the grain had sprouted and produced a crop,
  • then **the tares also appeared**.
    27 *So the servants of the owner came and said to him, 'Sir, did you not sow good seed in your field?*
  • **How then does it have tares?'**
28 He said to them, '**An enemy has done this**.' The servants said to him, 'Do you want us then to go and gather them up?' 29 But he said, 'No,
  • lest while you gather **up the tares you also uproot the wheat** with them.
30 Let both grow together until the harvest,
  • and at the time of harvest I will say to the reapers,
    ➢ "First **gather** together **the tares**
      • and **bind** them in bundles to
      • **burn** them,
    ➢ but gather the **wheat into my barn**."' **Matthew 13:24-30 (NKJV)**

Jesus has laid this parable out for us; we must exegete the passage understanding the **symbols** and **time frame**.

WHEN IS THE HARVEST?

"*Then Jesus sent the multitude away and went into the house. And His disciples came to Him, saying, **"Explain to us the parable of the tares of the field."***
37 He answered and said to them:

✔ *"He who sows the good seed is **the Son of Man**. 38*
✔ *The field is **the world**,*
✔ *the good seeds are **the sons of the kingdom**, but*
✔ *the tares are **the sons of the wicked one**. 39*
✔ *The enemy who sowed them is **the devil**,*
✔ *the harvest is **the end of the age**,*
✔ *and the reapers are **the angels**.*

*40 Therefore as **the tares** are*
   • *gathered and*
   • *burned in the fire,*
so it will be at the end of this age.
*41 **The Son of Man** will **send out His angels**, and*
they will **gather out of His kingdom**
   • *all things that offend,*
   • *and those who practice lawlessness,*
*42 and **will cast them into the furnace of fire**. There will be*
   • *wailing and gnashing of teeth.*
*43 Then **the righteous** will shine forth as the sun in **the kingdom of their Father**. He who has ears to hear, let him hear!* **Matthew 13:36-43 (NKJV)**

WHO ARE THOSE LEFT BEHIND IN THE BIBLE, SCRIPTURALLY?

When reading the passages, it is important to pay attention to the small words as well as the big ones:

There are several things that should draw our attention:

1. The Son of Man commands the reapers who are identified as the angels to let **both groups grow together**.
   a. Group-A the wheat: The Church (*Jews and gentiles*).
   b. Group-**B** the tares: (*The nation of Israel and unbelieving Gentiles*).

2. In verse 28, the servants asked a question; do you want us to go and pull them up (the tares)? No, He said. You might also uproot the wheat.
   a. The scholars may say, well yes this is dealing with judgment of the nations. Exactly.
   b. And there is no separation of the wheat and the tares. *Even so, the scholars have been teaching for centuries that the Church would be taken away first*.

3. In verses 30, the first group taken away by the reapers (angels) are:

      a. People in **group-B the tares**.
      b. People in **group-B** are **bound** in **bundles to be burned.**

But in all the *left behind novels* they show:
- believers being taken away (*rapture, caught-up*),
- and **unbelievers being left behind.**
- The biblical evidence does not substantiate the premise of unbelievers being left behind

4. The separation **time stamp** for these two groups is at the end of the **world** or **age, when CHRIST returns**.
5. It appears that someone has mixed these two events together and has been giving us the **wrong information**.
6. The reapers (angels) are instructed to gather group-A (wheat) into His barn.
7. The **barn** is symbolic of **the Kingdom of GOD**. At the time of Christ's return, these left behind believers, group A, goes into the kingdom (not up in the air), which is the beginning of the thousand-year millennium.
   - The symbolic language in verse 24 points to the **kingdom of God** which is a reference to the **Millennium Kingdom** which is about to be set up on earth.
8. There is still no Biblical evidence of a **pre-tribulation** rapture!

Obviously, Jesus has clearly given the reader a blow by blow as it relates to:
- the **players** (the wheat and the tares)
- the **time frame**
- the **outcome**
- **who will go first** and where **they will be taken.**

Question? Where is the Biblical writer and the passage that says **First** gather **the wheat**, the just, the righteous, the sheep, or the Church as a whole? Could it be in the so-called *lost books* of the Bible?

The Biblical conclusion:

- In all the ***left-behind*** movies the picture has been painted **wrong** for years, follow the Biblical text and let it be your **guide to truth**.

Although part of Ron Rhode's statement is true, we must always look for the small lie in any statement that is presented as evidence. In the garden of Eden, Satan told Eve, "ye shall not surely die" (KJV), likewise, the pre-tribulation view gives this same false sense of security. Some will ask, where is the lie? When you misinterpret the Scripture and say both groups are going back to heaven you have now drawn a false narrative that deceives the reader. According to Ron Rhodes:

> "The rapture is that glorious event in which Christ will descend from heaven, the dead in Christ will be resurrected, *and living Christians will be instantly translated into their resurrection bodies.* Both groups will be caught up to meet Christ in the air and taken back to heaven (1 Thessalonians 4:13-17; John 14:1-3; 1 Corinthians 15:51-54). *This means one generation of Christians will never pass through death's door. They will be alive on earth one moment; the next moment they will be with Christ in the air.*"[25]

- Those who teach a pre-tribulation rapture are **incorrect** in their teaching that there is a point where Christ returns before the second advent in the air to receive the church to Himself.

These are the lessons that Christ taught, and no scholar trumps the teachings of Christ!!! No One!

THE PARABLE OF THE GREAT DRAGNET: MATTHEW 13: 47-50:

Continuing to teach His disciples, the Lord uses a parable that relates to fishermen and how they cast out the net to draw in fish this is also in reference to how the gospel shall be preached to all people some will receive and become righteous and others will not and are unworthy.

---

[25] Ron Rhodes, Bible Prophecy Answer Book, Harvest House Publishers, 2017, p105

Notice, if the Church will follow the consistent pattern of our Lord, as He lays out the examples, He gives the Church enough detail to expel any false premise that He did not teach.

The parable is short and yet very impactful. The dragnet shall be brought to shore at the end of the age the angels shall separate the good from the bad at the end of the age when Christ returns.

Let us point out the obvious! There is no **pre-tribulation separation** that Christ spoke about to His followers (at least not in what has been written). So, if He did not teach it, and **the Holy Spirit** did not teach it, then it simply is not true.

The parable is explained in a way that His disciples, many who were fisherman, would clearly understand. Notice the underscoring message is the same as that in the parable of the *tares and the wheat* which the farmer would have understood:

> "Again, the **kingdom of heaven** is **like** unto a **net**, that was cast into the **sea**,
>   • and gathered of every kind: 48
> Which, **when it was full**, they drew to shore, and sat down, **and gathered**
>   • **the good into vessels**,
>   • but **cast the bad away.** 49
>
> So shall it be at **the end of the world**:
>   • **the angels** shall **come forth**,
>   ➤ and **sever** the **wicked** from among **the just**, 50
>   ➤ And shall **cast them** into **the furnace of fire**:
>   ➤ **there** shall be **wailing** and **gnashing of teeth**. 51
> Jesus saith unto them, **Have ye understood all these things?** They say unto him, Yea, Lord." **Matthew 13:47-51 (KJV)**

1. The fishermen would cast out their net into the sea to draw that which is good to eat. Of course, all sorts of fish and other objects could get caught in the net, and when they returned to the shore, they would **discard those things which were bad**.

2. Jesus says it so plainly that **at the end of the world His angels** (reapers) shall come and sever

the wicked (non-believers) from amongst the just (all believers).

3. The time frame is set, the workers are appointed, and there is no **pre-tribulation separation of any sort**.

These are the lessons that Christ taught. **Eschatology** is essential and the theme throughout the parables Jesus used in His teaching.

THE PARABLE OF THE TEN VIRGINS - MATTHEW 25:1-13:

As our Lord once again teaches, He sets His sights on what looks to be a group of righteous people who are waiting on the return of the groom. As the story unfolds, we learn that some from this group are not actually able to wait into the late hour for His return.

This is similar to how He had asked His disciples can you not pray and watch for an hour, but they all fell asleep and were not on their watch as they should have been.

In like manner when the groom returns many will be unprepared and without oil which is the substance that gives light to lead you down the path to the groom. Notice both groups are on the earth when He returns one is ready burning with oil being the light of the world the other has not found the path and have missed their opportunity to enter in.

The main theme in this Parable is to be prepared for the return of the Bridegroom:

> *"Then shall **the kingdom of heaven** be likened unto **ten virgins**, which **took their lamps**, and went forth **to meet the bridegroom**. 2*
> - *And **five of them were wise**,*
> - *and **five were foolish**. 3*
> *They that were **foolish***
> - *took their lamps, and **took no oil with them**: 4*
> *But the wise*
> - ***took oil** in their vessels with their lamps.*
>
> *5 While the **bridegroom tarried**, they all slumbered and slept. 6 And at midnight there was a cry made, Behold, the **bridegroom cometh**; go ye out to meet him. 7*

> *Then **all those virgins arose**,*
> - *and trimmed their lamps. 8*
>
> *And the **foolish***
> - *said unto **the wise**, Give us of your oil; for our lamps are gone out. 9*
>
> *But **the wise***
> - *answered, saying, Not so; lest there be not enough for **us** and **you**: but go ye rather to them that sell, and buy for yourselves. 10*
>
> *And **while** they went to buy, the **bridegroom came**;*
> *and **they** that **were ready***
> - ***went in** with **him** to **the marriage**: and the door was shut 11*
>
> *Afterward*
> - *came also **the other virgins**, saying, **Lord, Lord**, open to us. 12*
>
> *But **he** answered and said, Verily I say unto you, **I know you not**. 13 **Watch therefore**, for ye know neither **the** day nor **the** hour wherein **the Son of man cometh**.*" **Matthew 25:1-13 (KJV)**

Notice in his return **those** who were **prepared** went into the **supper**, it is a continuous **teaching of Christ** that there will be **two groups** of people at his **second coming**. There is No mention of **any** Pre-tribulation **separation**.

CHAPTER THREE

THE SHEEP AND THE GOAT - MATTHEW 25:31-46:

The Great Shepherd explains what will happen when He returns to judge all of mankind with His angels. Note the timeframe of this event; it is at the second advent of Christ. He says when He returns in all His glory. As the Lion, He will separate the sheep from the goats and these goats will go into eternal hellfire which we understand to be hell (Gehenna), but the sheep will go into the kingdom of God and why do the sheep go into the kingdom because of the works they were doing until His great return. They kept His command and worked even though they were persecuted, and they did not love their lives even until the death. Jesus is consistent with His message and there is absolutely no escape from His teachings.

> *"When **the Son of Man** comes in his glory, and **all the angels** with him, then he will sit on his glorious throne. 32*
> - *All **the nations will be gathered** before him,*
> - *and **he will separate them one from another**, just as a shepherd separates **the sheep** from **the goats**. 33*
> - *He will put **the sheep on his right** and **the goats on the left**.*
>
> *34 **Then the King will say to those on his right,***
> - *'Come, you who are blessed by my Father; **inherit the kingdom** prepared for you from the foundation of the world. 35*
> - *" 'For I was hungry and you gave me something to eat; I was thirsty and you gave me something to drink; I was a stranger and you took me in; 36 I was naked and you clothed me; I was sick and you took care of me; I was in prison and you visited me.'*
>
> *37 "**Then the righteous will answer him, 'Lord**, when did we see you hungry and feed you, or thirsty and give you something to drink? 38 When did we see you a stranger and take you in, or without clothes and clothe you? 39 When did we see you sick, or in prison, and visit you?'*
> - *40 "And **the King will answer them**, 'Truly I tell you, whatever you did for one of the least of these brothers and sisters of mine, you did for me.'*
>
> *41 "**Then he** will also say to **those on the left**,*
> - *'**Depart from me**, you who are cursed, **into the eternal fire** prepared for **the devil** and **his angels!** 42*

- *For I was hungry and you gave me nothing to eat; I was thirsty and you gave me nothing to drink; 43 I was a stranger and you didn't take me in; I was naked and you didn't clothe me, sick and in prison and you didn't take care of me.'*

44 **"Then they too will answer, 'Lord**, *when did we see you hungry, or thirsty, or a stranger, or without clothes, or sick, or in prison, and not help you?'*
45 *"Then he will answer them, 'I tell you, whatever you did not do for one of the least of these, you did not do for me.' 46*
- *"**And they will go away into eternal punishment**, but **the righteous into eternal life.**'"* **Matthew 25:31-46 (CSB)**

The storyline of the kingdom continues and has not changed or moved off course. Observe how consistent Jesus is with the Information He gives His followers.

The **time frame** is set at the beginning of the passage (verse 1), when He comes **in His glory.** Apostle Paul reveals this in **2ⁿᵈ Thessalonians** 1:7

> *"and to give you who are troubled rest with us when **the Lord Jesus is revealed from heaven with His mighty angels**, 8 in flaming fire **taking vengeance***
> - *on those who do not know God, and*
> - *on those who do not obey the gospel of our Lord Jesus Christ."*

1. Notice, all these events happen at the end of the tribulation period, when Christ is about to set up the **Millennium Kingdom**.
2. All nations are set before Him, and **He separates** the **sheep** and the **goats.** The same evidence that was exhibited in the parables that preceded this one. In this parable it is taught from the understanding of one who is a **shepherd**.
3. The sheep are going into the **kingdom on earth** also known as the **Millennium Kingdom,** and the **goats** into **everlasting punishment**. Where is the **separation** when the church is so called raptured?

CHRIST constantly taught the same message in all His parables. It is evident, some have not been using their ears to hear what the SPIRIT has revealed from the mouth of CHRIST to His Churches.

CHAPTER FOUR

THE SIGNS OF HIS COMING- MATTHEW 24:27-51:

The main message that must be understood are the truths as related to *the return of Christ* that should be carefully exegeted from the passage. We must hear what the Spirit is saying to the Churches. The Church should be looking for the signs that Christ Himself told us to look for. We should never practice the process of interpreting text in such a way as to introduce our own presuppositions, agendas, or biases. It is bad hermeneutics (eisegesis) when anyone reads into the text what is not there; and tries to predict the day or hour of Christ's return.

The Church should be constantly on watch and ready for the indication of Christ return. As his followers, it is imperative that we pay close attention to all the details especially when the Church (believers) see the antichrist sitting in the temple. If the Church were not going to be here on the earth when these things would occur, I doubt the Lord would have told us to look for them.

This message is not just for Israel; It is also for the church. Both groups will be around to see these events. The message is two-fold in many verses in the Bible.

> "For as the lightning cometh out of the **east**, and shineth even unto the **west**; so shall also **the coming of the Son of man be**. 28 For wheresoever the **carcase** is,
> - there will the eagles be gathered together.
>
> 29 **Immediately after the tribulation** of those days
> - shall the sun be darkened,
> - and the moon shall not give her light,
> - and the stars shall fall from heaven,
> - and the powers of the heavens shall be shaken: 30
> And then shall appear **the sign of the Son of man in heaven**:
> - and then shall **all the tribes of the earth** mourn,
>   - and **they shall see the Son of man coming** in **the clouds of heaven**
>   - with **power**
>   - and **great glory**.
> 31 And **he shall send his angels** with a great sound of a trumpet,
> - and **they shall gather together his elect**

- ○ from the four winds,
- ○ from one end of heaven to the other.

³² Now learn a parable of the fig tree;
When **his branch** is yet **tender**, and **putteth forth leaves**, ye know that summer is nigh: ³³ So likewise ye,
- when ye shall **see all these things**, know that it is near, even at the doors. ³⁴
- Verily I say unto you, This generation shall not pass, **till all these things be fulfilled**.

³⁵ Heaven and earth shall pass away,
- **but my words shall not pass away**. ³⁶
- But of that day and hour knoweth no man, no, not the angels of heaven, but **my Father only**. ³⁷
- But as the days of Noe were, **so shall also the coming of the Son of man be**. ³⁸
  - ○ For as in the days that were before the flood
  - ○ they were eating
  - ○ and drinking,
  - ○ marrying and giving in marriage,

until the day that Noe entered into the ark, ³⁹ And **knew not until the flood came**, and **took them all away**;
- ➤ **so shall also the coming of the Son of man be.**

⁴⁰ *Then shall two be in the field;*
- *the one shall be taken,*
- ***and the other left.***

⁴¹ *Two women shall be grinding at the mill;*
- *the one shall be taken,*
- ***and the other left.***

THE WICKED AND FAITHFUL SERVANTS

⁴² *Watch therefore: for ye know not what hour your Lord doth come.* ⁴³ *But know this,*
- *that if the goodman of the house had known in what watch the thief would come,*
  - ○ ***he would have watched***, *and would* ***not have suffered his house to be broken up.***

⁴⁴ *Therefore* ***be ye also ready***:
- *for in such an hour* ***as ye think not***
  - ○ ***the Son of man cometh.***

⁴⁵ *Who then is* ***a faithful and wise servant***,
- *whom his lord hath made ruler over his household,*
- *to give them meat in due season?*

⁴⁶ ***Blessed is that servant,***
- *whom his lord when he cometh shall find so doing.* ⁴⁷
- *Verily I say unto you, That he shall make him ruler over all his goods.*

*48 But and if that **evil servant** shall say in his heart,*
- *My lord delayeth his coming; 49*
  - *And shall **begin to smite** his fellowservants,*
  - *and **to eat and drink with the drunken;***

50 The lord of that servant shall come in a day when he looketh not for him, and in an hour that he is not aware of, 51
- *And shall cut him asunder,*
- *and appoint him his portion with the hypocrites:*
- *there shall be weeping and gnashing of teeth." **Matthew 24:27-51(KJV)***

As we read the verses and carefully look at the evidence
1. The *left-behind,* once again, are the **faithful and wise servants**, and **the foolish** are appointed their portion with the hypocrites.
2. Not only are those *left-behind* not removed, but Christ finds them working upon His return.
3. Notice, also at Christ's return, they are given a portion of authority for being obedient to His command we see this in **Matthew 25:23** His Lord said unto him, Well done, good and faithful servant; thou hast been faithful over a few things, I will make thee ruler over many things: enter thou into the joy of the Lord.

Here is something to think about, why isn't the rapture mentioned at all in the synoptic gospels?

The Signs Of His Coming- Matthew 24:27-51:

CHAPTER FIVE

CHRIST TEACHES ON THE SECOND COMING:

Christ taught about the two distinct groups on earth at His return.

The scholars (pre-tribulationist) have taught that the group that is taken, *as related to the pre-tribulation rapture*, is the group that goes up to heaven and that the other group, the unbelievers, are the left behind.

But when we allow Scripture to speak, the text reveals that the verses are painting a different and undeniable picture through the use of contextual criticism and word study we can prove and validate the exact message that was given to us by God.

> *"Even thus shall it be in **the day when the Son of man is revealed**. 31 In that day,*
> - *he which shall be upon the housetop,*
>   - *and his stuff in the house,*
>   - ***let him not come down to take it away:***
> - *and he that is in the field,*
>   - *let him likewise **not return back**.*
> 32 *Remember Lot's wife.* 33
> - *Whosoever **shall seek to save his life shall lose it**;*
> - *and whosoever **shall lose his life shall preserve it**.*
>
> 34 ***I tell you, in that night***
> - *there shall be two men in one bed;*
>   - the one shall be taken,
>   - ***and the other shall be left**. 35*
> - *Two women shall be grinding together;*
>   - the one shall be taken,
>   - ***and the other left**. 36*
> - *Two men shall be in the field;*
>   - the one shall be taken,
>   - ***and the other left**.*
> 37 *And they answered and said unto him, Where, Lord?*
> *And he said unto them, Wheresoever **the body is**,*
> - *thither will **the eagles be gathered together**."* **Luke 17:30-37 (KJV)**

When we exegete the text we are informed of the timeframe in the passage. The **{in that day}** *the return of Christ* is a reference to the second advent of Christ.

1. This passage warns **not to be concerned** with saving the things of this life, but to be prepared to sacrifice all and through this you will preserve your life.
2. The reference to {**that night**} is metaphorically a reference to a time when work stops.
3. This word **taken** in the Greek G-3880 **(paralambano) to take one captive NOT to carry into heaven.**

   ❖ The word in *1ˢᵗ Thessalonian's 4:17* in the Greek G-726- **harpazo which is to snatch out or away.**

   > "Then we which are alive and remain shall be **caught up** together with them in the clouds, to meet the Lord in the air: and so shall we ever be with the Lord. **1ˢᵗ Thessalonians 4:17(KJV)**

   ❖ The people **taken** (*Luke 17:30-37*) are **captive** to be **destroyed** and not **taken up to be rescued** from **tribulation**. Main point the time frame for this event is at the **RETURN** of Christ.

4. **Where** is the place that these **people** are **taken** to? **Where** is the place that **the eagles** will be **gathered?**

   > *"And I saw an angel standing in the sun; and he cried with a loud voice, **saying to all the fowls that fly in the midst of heaven**,*
   > - ***Come and gather yourselves together unto the supper of the great God**; 18 That ye may **eat***
   >   - ***the flesh of kings**,*
   >   - *and **the flesh of captains**,*
   >   - *and **the flesh of mighty men**,*
   >   - *and **the flesh** of horses, and of them that sit on them,*
   >   - *and **the flesh of all men**, both free and bond, both small and great.*
   > *19 And I saw **the beast, and the kings of the earth, and their armies**, gathered together to **make war against** him that sat on **the horse, and against his army**."* **Revelation 19:17-19(KJV)**

   Notice:
   '"And they answered and said to Him, "Where, Lord?"

So He said to them, "Wherever **the body** is,
there **the eagles**
will be **gathered together**."' Luke 17:37 (NKJV)

"'And they said to him, "Where, Lord?" He said to them,
"Where **the corpse** is,
there **the vultures**
will **gather**." Luke 17:37(ESV)

5. Scripture interprets Scripture, and the Scripture, without a doubt, reveals that those who are taken in these verses are not raptured up to heaven and the **LEFT BEHIND** are **all believers** who are about to go into the **Millennium Kingdom**.

According to Jerome Smith's The Ultimate Cross-Reference Treasury (UCRT)[26] notes on Luke 17: 30-37:

❖ **one shall be taken**: This is not the rapture, but the second advent, for here those that are taken are destroyed *(*Mat_8:12; +*Mat_13:30; +*Mat_13:41; Mat_22:13; +Mat_24:41)*.
  o **Taken**: The "**taking**" here and in +Mat_24:40, is not the rapture of the church, **but the gathering out of all things that offend described in the parable of the wheat and tares** (and thus parallel **to the destruction of the wicked that were "taken" in the flood of Noah**, Mat_24:39), (+*Mat_13:30; Jer_11:11, Mic_4:12).
  • **the body**: The word G-4983 σωμα here must signify the same as πτωμα, G-4430 a **dead carcase**, in Mat_24:28, by which is intended the Jewish nation, which was
  • morally and judicially dead,
  • doomed to be devoured by the Roman armies, called eagles, partly from their strength and fierceness, and partly from their military ensigns, which were gold or silver eagles. The Roman fury pursued these wretched men wherever they were found: see the horrible account in Josephus, Bel. l. vii. c. 2, 6, 9-11, **Eze_39:11-15, **Dan_7:11, +*#Mat_24:28, Rev_19:18,

---

[26] The Ultimate Cross-Reference Treasury is based upon The New Treasury of Scripture Knowledge Copyright © 1992 by Jerome H. Smith and Nelson's Cross Reference Guide to the Bible © 2007 by Jerome H. Smith. Produced under arrangement with Thomas Nelson, Inc., P.O. Box 141000, Nashville, TN 37214.

- Whatever interpretation and application is made here of the term "body," must consistently apply equally to the term "carcass" used in +*#Mat_24:28,
    - To suggest the body is that of Christ, or believers, or **the nation Israel**, does not harmonize with Scripture.
    - Rather, suggesting that "**body**" and "**carcass**" refer to *the defeated armies gathered against Jerusalem at the end of the tribulation described* in Eze_39:17-21, seems to fit precisely, and is no doubt the event Christ is alluding to, reinforced by the mention of "eagles" directly in this connection, for the "feathered fowl" are invited to feast upon the carnage after that great battle (Eze_39:17).

        "'Son of man, this is what the Lord God says: Tell every kind of bird and all the wild animals, 'Assemble and come! Gather from all around to my sacrificial feast that I am slaughtering for you, a great feast on the mountains of Israel; you will eat flesh and drink blood. 18 You will eat the flesh of mighty men and drink the blood of the earth's princes: rams, lambs, male goats, and all the fattened bulls of Bashan. 19 You will eat fat until you are satisfied and drink blood until you are drunk, at my sacrificial feast that I have prepared for you. 20 At my table you will eat your fill of horses and riders, of mighty men and all the warriors. This is the declaration of the Lord God.'" **Ezekiel 39:17-20(CSB)**

    - To suggest that eagles here represent the Romans is not supported by the context, for the Romans are not otherwise alluded to in this passage, and the fall of Jerusalem in A.D. 70 is not the subject of this prophecy, for here these events take place at the second advent, when "the Son of man shall be revealed" (Luk_17:30).

WHO ARE THE SAINTS THAT RETURN WITH CHRIST?

There is only one group that the Bible says will return with Christ. Time to get straight to the point; There are too many sermons, lectures, books, and movies that programmed us to believe that **the saints** are going to return with Christ on white horses at the end of the tribulation.

Yes, saints are holy ones; and yes, saints / holy ones will return with Christ.

The problem! You cannot ignore context and bring about the clear intended meaning of a passage in the Word of God.

Context brings out the clear meaning of the passages given to help us determine *the who* is being referred to as, the word, "saints."

Studying the verses, closely, illustrates that the word **saint** is applied to *believers,* **angels,** *and Christ.*

> Let's start out laying the groundwork for this argument. Always define your terms: H-2429 chayil (Aramaic) is defined **an army of strength**. In the book of Daniel (*Daniel 4:35*), Scripture mentions *God's army* which is in heaven.

This is worth noting, because some say the saints **that return with CHRIST** are *human saints* on white horses and dressed in white apparel.

If we follow the verses in context, the readers will see that there is no mention of human saints doing any work or fighting during the tribulation period, but **Only our Lord and Savior and His army of Angels.** Which we will be pointing out **verse by verse**.

> *"' The enemy that sowed them is the devil; the harvest is **the end of the world;** and **the reapers are the angels**. 40 As therefore the tares are gathered and burned in the fire; so shall it be in the end of this world. 41 The Son of man shall **send forth his angels**, and they shall gather out of his **kingdom** all things that offend, and them which do iniquity; 42 **And shall cast them into a furnace of fire**: there shall be wailing and gnashing of teeth. 43 Then shall the righteous shine forth as the sun in the kingdom of their Father. **Who hath ears to hear, let him hear**."'* **Matthew 13:39-43 (KJV)**

*'" And **he shall send his angels** with a great sound of a trumpet, and **they shall gather together his elect** from the four winds, from one end of heaven to the other."'* **Matthew 24:31(KJV)**

The passages above were noticeably clear as to who God is using and the job they will be performing.

- The time of the event is clear also.

Question, where are the **human saints** and what **work** are, they **doing**?

This would be a great place to see those **human saints** returning with CHRIST on their horse's doing some kind of task. But there is not a single utterance of such an occurrence in the Scripture. **Also,** the "**these" who are elect are gathered rather than taken**, where are they going? The sheep are gathered into the barn or better yet into the Millennium Kingdom, not into heaven to meet the LORD in the air. He has returned and we see no mention of any **pre-tribulation rapture**, Or any separation.

RETURN OF CHRIST: MATTHEW 16:24-28

Pay close attention to the details that the disciples recorded.

One of the main things that should be observed from this passage is that faithful servants (*the Church*) are called to lose their lives or as the passage is displaying forfeit the things of the world with a strong possibility of losing one's life. This same message is presented in the book of *Luke 17:33*.

Another reason for visiting this passage is because Christ is returning, but there are myths that must be dispelled about who is returning with Him, so that

- our fellow brothers and sisters are not fooled by the cunning craftiness of men who change the doctrine of Christ.
- the Church is not given a false sense of security.
- the body of Christ will not be looking for a return and participation in a process the Church has not been made apart or included.

'" Then said Jesus unto his disciples, If any man will come after me, let him deny himself, and take up his cross, and follow me. 25 For

> *whosoever will save his life shall lose it: and whosoever will lose his life for my sake shall find it. 26 For what is a man profited, if he shall gain the whole world, and lose his own soul? or what shall a man give in exchange for his soul? 27 **For the Son of man shall come in the glory of his Father with his angels; and then he shall reward every man according to his works**. 28 Verily I say unto you, There be some standing here, which shall not taste of death, till they see the Son of man coming in his kingdom."'*
> **Matthew 16:24-28 (KJV)**

In these verses we see Christ has returned and judgment has come upon men where can we verify or cross reference this event ?

> *"'Whosoever therefore shall be ashamed of me and of my words in this adulterous and sinful generation; of him also shall the Son of man be ashamed, **when he cometh in the glory of his Father with the holy angels**.'"* **Mark 8:38 (KJV)**

> *"'And he said unto them, Verily I say unto you, That **there be some of them that stand here, which shall not taste of death, till they have seen the kingdom of God come with power**.'"* **Mark 9:1 (KJV)**

Now we see the Messiah has returned and judgment has come. **His *angels* are doing their appointed Jobs. Notice** in the last verse; what is Jesus talking about that *some will not taste death until they see the kingdom*?

This is clearly a reference to believers being present when the Kingdom of GOD comes to the earth. We should always take note of the messages that Jesus teach and never allow ourselves to be influenced by the speculative ideas of men which contradict the direct teachings of Christ.

Of course, when Christ comes and sets up the kingdom, believers will enter the thousand-year millennium but they will still be able to die, this is the reason the statement was made. Also,
> **if**
> > He is coming to separate
> **then**
> > ***NO previous separation*** has occurred.
> **If**
> > it has previously occurred,
> **then**

we should see it in the text.

*"**Immediately after the tribulation** of those days shall the sun be darkened, and the moon shall not give her light, and the stars shall fall from heaven, and the powers of the heavens shall be shaken: 30 **And then shall appear the sign of the Son of man in heaven**: and then shall all the tribes of the earth mourn, and they shall **see the Son of man coming in the clouds of heaven with power and great glory**. 31 And **he shall send his angels with a great sound of a trumpet**, and **they shall gather together his elect** from the four winds, from one end of heaven to the other."* **Matthew 24:29-31 (KJV)**

THE TRIBULATION AND THE SECOND COMING OF CHRIST: MARK 13:19-27

Observing the book of Mark and the evidence that is revealed, there is an astounding number of discrepancies in what the scholars have been teaching for the last one hundred and forty years. In comparison to that which the disciples taught when Christ returns and who will accompany Him after the tribulation.

A proper reading of text reveals:
- These who are the elect are on the earth, now. This is a term given to believers not just those in Israel.
- Furthermore, Israel will be safe in the mountains in Jerusalem. These elects are gathered from all around the earth which lets us know that the tribulation period has more than just the twelve tribes of Jacob being saved by the return of Christ.

*"**For in those days** shall be affliction, such as was not from the beginning of the creation which God created unto this time, neither shall be. 20 **And except that the Lord had shortened those days,** no flesh should be saved: but for the elect's sake, whom he hath chosen, he hath shortened the days. 21 And then if any man shall say to you, **Lo, here is Christ; or, lo, he is there; believe him not:** 22 For false Christs and false prophets shall rise, and shall shew signs and wonders, to seduce, if it were possible, even the elect. 23 But take ye heed: behold, I have **foretold** you all things. 24 But in those days, after that tribulation, the sun shall be darkened, and the moon shall not give her light, 25 And the stars of heaven shall fall, and the powers that are in heaven shall be shaken. **26 And then shall they see the Son of man coming in the***

clouds with great power and glory. 27 And then shall he send his angels, and shall gather together his elect from the four winds, from the uttermost part of the earth to the uttermost part of heaven." **Mark 13:19-27 (KJV)**

The scripture continues to repeat the same evidence seen in several books of the Bible, also the words of the Messiah are repeatedly and constantly reinforcing the same information in our minds. How many times does it have to be said before the Biblical reader believe it?

Notice the signs that Christ says you will see before He returns with His holy angels.
Sun darkened, **moon** not giving its light, **stars** from heaven falling; **all these things are clues to His return.**

Also, He gave a warning about **false teacher's** telling you look the Christ is here or there. He warns that they will tell you he is in places that **He will not be**.

These warnings are here so that *His Church* will not be deceived and start looking for Him at a time that He has not said in His teachings. **So please be watching and prepared**!

TRUE COST OF DISCIPLESHIP - LUKE 9:23-27

*"And he said to them all, If any man will come after me, **let him deny himself**, and take up his cross daily, and follow me. 24 For whosoever will save his life shall lose it: **but whosoever will lose his life for my sake, the same shall save it**. 25 For what is a man advantaged, if he gain the whole world, and lose himself, or be cast away? 26 **For whosoever shall be ashamed of me and of my words, of him shall the Son of man be ashamed, when he shall come in his own glory,** and in **his Father's**, and **of the holy angels**. 27 But I tell you of a truth, there be some standing here, which shall not taste of death, till they see the kingdom of God."* **Luke 9:23-27(KJV)**

Notice, what Christ said when He was upon the earth; who would the FATHER send to help Him if He needed help.

*"And, behold, one of them which were with Jesus stretched out his hand, **and drew his sword,** and struck a servant of the high priest's, and smote off his ear. 52 Then said Jesus unto him, **Put up again thy sword into his place:** for all they that take the sword shall perish with the sword. 53 **Thinkest thou that I cannot***

now pray to my Father, and he shall presently give me more than twelve legions of angels?" **Matthew 26:51-53 (KJV)**

Doing the simple math: How many is in a legion? 6000 times 12 equals 72,000 angels.

Next, we should consider how many angels we see standing around the throne of GOD during tribulation and where should we look? How about

"And I beheld, and I heard the voice of **many angels round about the throne** *and the beasts and the elders:* **and the number of them was ten thousand times ten thousand, and thousands of thousands;** **Revelation 5:11(KJV)**

Brothers and sisters, this is an innumerable number of angels. The question remains the same. Where is the **scripture** that shows **humans** coming back with **Jesus**?

THE SECOND COMING OF CHRIST: 2ND THESSALONIANS 1:4-9

Reviewing the evidence, 1st Thessalonians chapter one happens to be one of the chapters that pre-tribulation adherents use to say that the Church does not go through the tribulation period.

According to the way this chapter reads, *Paul says that Christ will take vengeance on those who were persecuting the Church at His return with His holy angels from heaven.*

It is evident that the Apostle Paul's writings do not agree with the scholars, of today, who quote each other on the pre-tribulation rapture. Paul received his revelation from Christ, and he and Christ are on one accord; so how did the teachings of today get so far removed from the truth?

"Therefore, we ourselves boast about you among God's churches — about your perseverance and faith in all the persecutions and afflictions that you are enduring. 5 It is clear evidence of God's righteous judgment that you will be counted worthy of God's kingdom,
- *for which you also are suffering, 6*
- *since it is just for God to repay with affliction those who afflict you 7*
- *and to give relief to you who are afflicted, along with us.*
This will take place at the revelation of the Lord Jesus from heaven with his powerful angels, *8 when* **he takes vengeance** *with flaming fire*
- *on those who don't know God*
- *and on those who don't obey the gospel of our Lord Jesus.*

CHRIST Teaches On The Second Coming:

*9 They will pay **the penalty of eternal destruction** from the Lord's presence and from his glorious strength"* **2nd Thessalonians 1:4-9 (KJV) (CSB)**

We observe that the Lord has returned, and vengeance is falling on the unjust, but there still is no mention of human interaction during His return.

1. Notice in verse 5 that it says you will be counted worthy of the kingdom. This is addressed to the Church if they are raptured this would not apply.
2. Verse 6 says God is repaying those who afflict you, how can this be possible if the Church is already gone? We should never miss an opportunity to shed light on the whole subject at hand.
3. Verse 7 says you (who are troubled) are receiving this relief at the revelation of Christ, that is at His return with His mighty angels (not humans). Also known as the Second Advent. The affliction that the church is receiving is lifted at the return of Christ when He starts to afflict those who were persecuting the Church. How could this be possible if the church were already raptured?
4. Verse 8 says when He takes vengeance on those who do not know Him or obey the gospel.
   a. Based on the verse, it is not referring to you who believe in HIS NAME:
      - NO WRATH FOR YOU,
      - AND NO EARLY DEPARTURE EITHER.

CHRIST Teaches On The Second Coming:

CHAPTER SIX

THE SEALS ARE BEING OPENED: REVELATION 6:8-11

As we approach this chapter, it is especially important to receive the message that we are given. John has given us the direct commandment from the Lord that those who are presently in heaven should stay at the altar of God until the rest of their fellow servants should be killed as they were who kept the Word of God and had the testimony of God. We see this information addressed in **Revelation 1:9** which is also addressed to the Church. If the message is that they stay at the altar, how are they returning with Christ? This would be a direct contradiction of scripture. Based on the Biblical evidence presented, we should conclude that only the angels will be returning with Christ.

> *"And I looked, and behold a pale horse: and his name that sat on him was Death, and Hell followed with him. And power was given unto them over the fourth part of the earth, to kill with sword, and with hunger, and with death, and with the beasts of the earth.*
> *9 And when he had opened the fifth seal, I saw under the altar the souls of them that were slain for the word of God, and for the testimony which they held: 10 And they cried with a loud voice, saying, How long, O Lord, holy and true, **dost thou not judge and avenge our blood on them that dwell on the earth?** 11 And white robes were given unto every one of them; and it was said unto them, that **they should rest** yet **for a little season, until their fellowservants also and their brethren**, that **should be killed** as they were, should be fulfilled."* **Revelation 6:8-11 (KJV)**

The next question that should be asked is **when does the killing stop?** The Scripture addresses this question for us.

> *"And **except those days should be shortened, there should no flesh be saved**: but for the elect's sake those days shall be shortened."* **Matthew 24:22 (KJV)**

These **saints** are told to **rest** (*6:11*) at the **altar of GOD** until all is **complete** with this **wrath** that **Christ brings on the unbelievers**.

1. If they are told to rest until the killing is stopped, when do they **get** bodies and **get** the horses to return with CHRIST?

2. Scriptures used improperly to support the pre-tribulation premises have contextual issues. Far too long, they have used good Biblical evidence in an incorrect manner, which we are about to clear up.

3. Do not forget the **premise**, that teachers and scholars have said that we **return with Christ on horses.**

The Biblical evidence proves that only angels and Christ return this way (on horses): let the Scriptures speak.

WHO ARE THE ONES RETURNING WITH CHRIST? REVELATION 9:12-21

> "One woe is past; and, behold, there come two woes more hereafter.
>
> 13 And **the sixth angel** sounded, and I heard a voice from the four horns of the golden altar which is before God, 14 Saying to the sixth angel which had **the trumpet, Loose the four angels which are bound in the great river Euphrates.** 15
> - And the four angels were loosed, which were prepared for an hour, and a day, and a month, and a year, for to slay the third part of men. 16
> - And the number of the army of the horsemen were two hundred thousand thousand: and I heard the number of them. 17
> - And **thus I saw the horses in the vision, and them that sat on them,** having breastplates of fire, and of jacinth, and brimstone: and the heads of the horses were as the heads of lions; and out of their mouths issued fire and smoke and brimstone. 18 By these three was the third part of men killed, by the fire, and by the smoke, and by the brimstone, which issued out of their **mouths.**
>
> 19 **For their power is in their mouth, and in their tails:** for their tails were like unto serpents, and had heads, and with them they do hurt. 20 And the rest of the men which were not killed by these plagues yet repented not of the works of their hands, that they should not worship devils, and idols of gold, and silver, and brass, and stone, and of wood: which neither can see, nor hear, nor walk: 21 **Neither repented they of their murders, nor of their sorceries, nor of their fornication, nor of their thefts.**" Revelation 9:12-21 (KJV)

These verses are happening as the tribulation is taking place, the point of this section is to see who returns with CHRIST, where are the human saints that return with the Messiah? Verse by verse line by line we do not find any evidence of this in the Scriptures.

THE SEVEN LAST PLAGUES - REVELATION 15:1-8

"Then I saw another great and awe-inspiring sign in heaven: **seven angels** *with the* **seven last plagues;** *for with them* **God's wrath** *will* **be completed.** *2*
- *I also saw something like a sea of glass mixed with fire, and those who had won the victory over the beast, its image, and the number of its name, were standing on the sea of glass with harps from God.* *3*

They sang the song of God's servant Moses and the song of the Lamb: Great and awe-inspiring are your works, Lord God, the Almighty; just and true are your ways, **King of the nations.** *4 Lord, who will not fear and glorify your name? For you alone are holy. All the nations will come and worship before you because your righteous acts have been revealed. 5 After this I looked, and the heavenly temple — the tabernacle of testimony —was opened.*
- *6* **Out of the temple came the seven angels** *with* **the seven plagues, dressed in pure, bright linen,** *with golden sashes wrapped around their chests.*

7 **One** *of the four* **living creatures** *gave* **the seven angels seven golden bowls filled with the wrath of God** *who lives forever and ever. 8 Then the temple was filled with smoke from the glory of God and from his power, and no one could enter the temple until the seven plagues of the seven angels were completed.* **Revelation 15: 1-8 (CSB)**

Starting at verse one, the seven angels are given the task of completing the seven last plagues.
1. Verse 2:
    a. This sea of glass where is it at?
    b. Where are these people congregating?
    They are at the throne of God in heaven. Reference verse **Revelation 4:6**
2. In verse six: This is where we see the angels dressed in white apparel, **now we know that Human saints (*6:11*) and Angels (*15:6*) are both dressed in the righteousness of GOD**.
    - Does this mean that **both groups** are **returning** with **Christ** at His return?

The Scripture has already concluded that **they were told to rest.**

WHO ARE THE SAINTS RETURNING WITH CHRIST? REVELATION 19:1-10

The myth that is being exposed in this section is that pre-tribulation adherents believe *the Church which has been raptured is returning with Christ on white horses.*
Can this view be substantiated when Scripture is rightly divided?

> "**After this I heard something like the loud voice of a vast multitude in heaven,** saying, Hallelujah! Salvation, glory, and power belong to our God, 2 because his judgments are true and righteous, because **he has judged the notorious prostitute** who corrupted the earth with her sexual immorality; and **he has avenged the blood of his servants** that was **on her hands.** 3 second time they said, **Hallelujah!** Her smoke ascends forever and ever! 4 Then the twenty-four elders and **the four living creatures** fell down and **worshiped God, who is seated on the throne,** saying, Amen! **Hallelujah!** 5 **A voice came from the throne,** saying, Praise our God, all his servants, and the ones who fear him, both small and great! 6 Then I heard something like the voice of a vast multitude, like the sound of cascading waters, and like the rumbling of loud thunder, saying, Hallelujah, because our Lord God, the Almighty, reigns! 7 Let us be glad, rejoice, and give him glory, **because the marriage of the Lamb has come,** and his bride has prepared herself. 8 **She was given fine linen to wear, bright and pure. For the fine linen represents the righteous acts of the saints.** 9 Then he said to me, "**Write: Blessed are those invited to the marriage feast of the Lamb!**" He also said to me, "These words of God are true." 10 Then I fell at his feet to worship him, but he said to me, "Don't do that! I am a fellow servant with you and your brothers and sisters who hold firmly to the testimony of Jesus. Worship God, because the testimony of Jesus is the spirit of prophecy." **Revelation 19:1-10(CSB)**

There are many who teach that the **saints** in *Revelation 19:1-10* are included among the **armies that return with CHRIST** on white horses. Based on proper hermeneutics, there is no way that can be correct.

Here is the plane truth about verses 19:1-10 chronologically **they happen after verses** 11-21.

1. The first half of **Revelation 19:1-10** is about the marriage supper of the LORD, and His conquering over the harlot system.
2. Also notice in verse 5 where the voice is coming **from the throne** which means **they are in heaven**.
3. The latter half of **Revelation 19:11-21** is about CHRIST returning on the white horse and victory over the **antichrist** and the **false prophet** which happen **at the end of the tribulation**. No Scripture verifies any humans returning to the earth until the **resurrection of the just** which happens in the next chapter.

*"He seized the dragon, that ancient serpent who is the devil and Satan, and bound him for **a thousand years**. 3 He threw him into the abyss, closed it, and put a seal on it so that he would no longer deceive the nations until the thousand years were completed. After that, he must be released for a short time. 4 Then I saw **thrones**, and **people** seated **on them** who were **given authority to judge**. I also saw **the souls** of those **who had been beheaded because of their testimony about Jesus** and because of **the word of God**, who had not worshiped the beast or his image, and **who had not** accepted **the mark on their foreheads** or their hands. **They came to life and reigned with Christ for a thousand years**. 5 The **rest of the dead** did not come to life until the thousand years were completed. This is the first resurrection. 6 Blessed and holy is the one who shares in **the first resurrection!** The **second death** has **no power over them**, but they will be priests of God and of Christ, and **they will reign with him for a thousand years**."* **Revelation 20:2-6 (CSB)**

Notice who **returns with CHRIST** and when the **first resurrection** occurs. This is the first mass resurrection at the end of tribulation. How can the first massive resurrection have happened in 1st **Thessalonians 4:13-18?**

The first resurrection is expressed in the word of God as a series of resurrections appointed for the righteous in Christ.

We see a couple of events that play out dealing with what is known as the resurrection of the just. For example:

- After Christ, the two witnesses in Revelation chapter 11:11-12.

- The mass resurrection in Revelation chapter 20:1-4.
- And the resurrection of all those who will die in the Millennium period who will be raptured with Christ at the end of the Millennium (**1 Corinthians 15:50-52**).

Some will ask, why isn't 1st Thessalonians 4:13-17 a resurrection passage? Notice, It Is the resurrection of Revelation chapter 20:1-4.

CHAPTER SEVEN

THE WRATH OF GOD

We are told by pre-tribulation adherents that we escape the wrath of God. We should all agree with the Scripture in the context in which the message has been given in light of all Scripture as a whole. From a Biblical perspective, the Church adherents should be investigating and seeking illumination on

- Who exactly does the Word of God in context says shall receive GOD'S wrath?
- Are believers still on the earth as God's wrath is poured out on unbelievers or have believers been previously removed (raptured)?

ARE CHRISTIANS EXCLUDED FROM WRATH?

The Bible says that Christians are excluded from *divine wrath* and Pre-tribulationists use the following verse to support their view that the Church will be raptured before The Great Tribulation:

> *"and to wait for his Son from heaven, whom he raised from the dead — Jesus, who rescues us from the coming wrath."* **1 Thessalonians 1:10 (CSB)**

Now using contextual criticism – we will see if their argument stands up to the evidence given in the text.

Let us critique the text:

> *"Paul, Silvanus, and Timothy: **To the church** of the Thessalonians in God the Father and the Lord Jesus Christ. Grace to you and peace. 2 We always thank God for all of you, making mention of you constantly in our prayers. 3 We recall, in the presence of our God and Father, your work **produced by faith**, your labor motivated by love, and your endurance inspired by hope in our Lord Jesus Christ."* **1 Thessalonians 1-3 (CSB)**

Notice verses 1 through 3 is clear the chapter is written to the church and the subject is their faith.
"For we know, brothers and sisters loved by God, that he has chosen you, 5 because our gospel did not come to you in word only, but also in power, in the Holy Spirit, and with full assurance.

> *You know how we lived among you for your benefit, 6 and you yourselves became imitators of us and of the Lord when, in spite of severe persecution, you welcomed the message with joy from the Holy Spirit. 7 As a result, you became an example to all the believers in Macedonia and Achaia."* **1 Thessalonians 4-7(CSB)**

Verses 4 through 7 have demonstrated that the Church in Thessalonica **was chosen by God**. The Holy Spirit was working through them; and they were operating according to their calling despite **suffering and persecution.** They were displaying the righteousness of Christ.

> *"For the word of the Lord rang out from you, not only in Macedonia and Achaia, but in every place that your faith in God has gone out. Therefore, we don't need to say anything, 9 for they themselves report what kind of reception we had from you: how you turned to God from idols to serve the living and true God 10 and to wait for his Son from heaven, whom he raised from the dead — **Jesus, who rescues us from the coming wrath**."* **1 Thessalonians 8-10(CSB)**

Let's pay close attention to the word delivered or rescued, this is not referring to you being delivered from the Great Tribulation. This deliverance is in reference to their current position in Christ the context of the text determines the usage of the word.

Notice that the Scriptures, when read in the context and order of their delivery, we learn that God uses the word (**Ryomai or delivered**) to a person's current state in Christ and He doesn't use it in reference to one who is escaping From The Great Tribulation.

The word is being applied to one who is delivered:
1. From the hands of their enemies that they may serve Him.
2. From the greater death which is total separation from Christ. The text is not implying that they are delivered from the first death or any death.
3. From the practice of sin and darkness through Christ. Even so it is still possible to receive persecution, affliction, and even death. Endurance through Christ places the believer in the right position.

This is a positional Deliverance.

G 4506 rhyomai[27]
Outline of Biblical Usage
I.   to draw to one's self, *to rescue*, *to deliver*
II.   the deliverer

Here are four examples:

- *"To grant us that we, **Being delivered** from the hand of our enemies, Might serve Him without fear,"* **Luke 1:74 (NKJV)**
- *"who delivered us from so great a death, and does deliver us; in whom **we trust that He will still deliver us**,"* **2 Corinthians 1:10 (NKJV)**
- *"**He has delivered us from the power of darkness** and conveyed us into the kingdom of the Son of His love,"* **Colossians 1:13 (NKJV)**
- *"persecutions, afflictions, which happened to me at Antioch, at Iconium, at Lystra—what persecutions I endured. **And out of them all the Lord delivered me**."* **2 Timothy 3:11 (NKJV)**

Notice the text in context shows that God **delivers the saints** from **the wrath** to come because of their **faith in Jesus Christ**.

The problem is pre-tribulationists argue that *the wrath* that comes on the earth to test a man cannot be applied to you.

However, as believers we should agree that:
- God's wrath does not fall upon the believers, and the Scripture is not referring to delivery of the believer from the **wrath of *God***.
- Christ through His death on the cross has delivered the believer into a present state in the Kingdom of God.

Based on a proper reading of the text:
A. The Church is currently delivered, and the great tribulation has not occurred.
B. The text is not referring to the great tribulation which is discussed in the book of Revelation which was not written until approximately 96 A.D.

---

[27] https://www.blueletterbible.org/lang/lexicon/lexicon.cfm?Strongs=G4506&t=KJV

C. The problem is pre-tribulation adherents argue that this is the wrath of The Great Tribulation. The verse is about a believer not receiving any wrath that could occur from God against any believers, such as going to Hell or any judgment when Christ returns.

D. The book of 1st Thessalonians is consistently addressing the second coming of Christ not the rapture of the Church.

Please read the whole book with these scriptures in mind. 1st Thessalonians 1:10, 2:19, 3:13, 4:15, 5:2; contextually all these verses are about the second coming of Christ not a rapture.

IS THERE AN ESCAPE PLAN FOR THE CHURCH?

Believers are exempt from the wrath of God recorded in:

*"Because **you have kept** my command to endure, I will also **keep you from the hour of testing** that is going to come on the whole world to test those who live on the earth."* **Revelation 3:10 (CSB)**

Pre-tribulation adherents use **Revelation 3:10** as an example to support their premise that God **keeps** the Church from any wrath during the great tribulation. The word **keep** in the verse does not encompass a rapturing away.

G5083[28] tēreō in the following manner: **keep** (57x), reserve (8x), observe (4x), watch (2x), preserve (2x), keeper (1x), hold fast (1x).

Outline of Biblical Usage

I. to attend to carefully, take care of
   A. to guard
   B. metaph. to keep, one in the state in which he is
   C. to observe
   D. to reserve: to undergo something

Examples:
- *"And now I am no more in the world, but these are in the world, and I come to thee. Holy Father, **keep** through thine own name those whom thou hast given me, that they may be one, as we are."* **John 17:11 (KJV)**

---

[28] https://www.blueletterbible.org/lang/lexicon/lexicon.cfm?Strongs=G5083&t=KJV

- *"While I was with them in the world, I **kept** them in thy name: those that thou gavest me I have **kept**, and none of them is lost, but the son of perdition; that the scripture might be fulfilled."* **John 17:12 (KJV)**
- "I pray not that thou shouldest take them out of the world, but that thou shouldest keep them from the evil." **John 17:15 (KJV)**

The verse explains this as a trial that will come on the whole world to test their faith, but believers **who endure and persevere are kept by Christ**.

This has nothing to do with God bringing wrath on the church, neither is it a message of an escape plan for the church.

Using contextual criticism let's see if the chapter supports the premise of their argument,

"you are being raptured away, so that you don't have to go through the Great tribulation,"

which they infer is the wrath of God.

"*Write to the angel of the church in Philadelphia: Thus says the Holy One, the true one, the one who has the key of David,*
- ***who opens*** *and no one will **close**, and*
- ***who closes*** *and no one **opens**: 8*

I know your works.
- *Look, I have placed before you an open door that no one can close **because you have but little power**;*
- *yet you have kept my word and have not denied my name. 9*

Note this:
- ***I will make*** *those from the synagogue of Satan, who claim to be Jews and are not, but are lying —*
  - ***I will make*** *them come and bow down at your feet,*
  - *and **they will know** that **I have loved you**.*
- "*Because **you have kept my command to endure**,*
  - ***I will also keep you*** *from the hour of testing **that is going to come on the whole world to test those who live on the earth**. " **Revelation 3:7-9 (CSB)***

Notice verses 7 through 10 are addressing the Church (***Jews and gentiles***) on the earth and acknowledges that even though it has little power it will persevere and endure until **Christ returns**. The Synagogue of Satan is the persecutor of the Church on the earth.

> *11 I am coming soon. Hold on to what you have, so that no one takes your crown. 12 "The one who conquers I will make a pillar in the temple of my God, and he will never go out again. I will write on him the name of my God and the name of the city of my God — the new Jerusalem, which comes down out of heaven from my God — and my new name. 13 "Let anyone who has ears to hear listen to what the Spirit says to the churches."*
> **Revelation 3:11-13 (CSB)**

In context, the verse points to the Church who was commanded "to keep", persevere, and "endure" while going through a great trial.

In verse 10 we see the Church (*Jews and gentiles*) on earth and verse 11, he says I am coming soon hold on to what you have.

What the Church is holding on to is their works (of verse 8) until Christ comes to the earth. These were not the resurrected saints, or the martyred saints, but those who were on earth. Notice the future tense of Christ saying "**I Will**" make him a pillar in the temple of My God. "**I will** Keep", "**I will** Make," and '**I will** Write."

The Church was commanded not to give up even if that meant not loving their lives unto the death.

a) **G-5281** hypomonē [29] "**endurance**" in context of the verse.

    Outline of Biblical Usage
- I.   steadfastness, constancy, endurance
  - A. in the NT the characteristic of a man who is not swerved from his deliberate purpose and his loyalty to faith and piety by even the greatest trials and sufferings
  - B. patiently, and steadfastly
- II. a patient, steadfast waiting for
- III. a patient enduring, sustaining, perseverance

Examples of endurance:

- *"If we are afflicted, it is for your comfort and salvation. If we are comforted, it is for your comfort, which produces in you **patient endurance** of the same sufferings that we suffer."* **2 Corinthians 1:6 (CSB)**
- *"Instead, as God's ministers, we commend ourselves in everything: by **great endurance**, by afflictions, by hardships, by difficulties,"* **2 Corinthians 6:4 (CSB)**

---

[29] https://www.blueletterbible.org/lang/lexicon/lexicon.cfm?Strongs=G5281&t=KJV (May 19,2020)

- *"For you need **endurance**, so that after you have done God's will, you may receive what was promised."* **Hebrews 10:36 (CSB)**
- *"If anyone is to be taken captive, into captivity he goes. If anyone is to be killed with a sword, with a sword he will Be killed. This calls **For***

  ***endurance** and faithfulness from the saints."* **Revelation 13:10 (CSB)**

b) **G-5083** tereo[30] – **"to keep"** in the context of this verse it means not to leave you, it does not mean to keep you from wrath. But to stay with you as you endure your trial.

Does this sound familiar? I will never leave or forsake you?

"we are persecuted **but not abandoned**; we are struck down **but not destroyed**. 10 We always carry the death of Jesus in our body, so that the life of Jesus may also be displayed in our body. 11 ***For we who live are always being given over to death for Jesus's sake***, so that Jesus's life may also be displayed in our mortal flesh. 12 So then, death is at work in us, but life in you. 13 And since we have the same spirit of faith in keeping with what is written, I believed, therefore I spoke, we also believe, and therefore speak. 14 **For we know that the one who raised the Lord Jesus will also raise us with Jesus and present us with you.**" **2 Corinthians 4:9-14 (CSB)**

*"Keep your life free from the love of money. Be satisfied with what you have, for he himself has said, **I will never leave you or abandon you**. 6 Therefore, we may boldly say, The Lord is my helper; I will not be afraid. **What can man do to me**?"* **Hebrews 13:5-6 (CSB)**

The Scripture backs up these claims.

"***Blessed is the one who endures trials***,
- *because when he has stood the test,*
  - ***he will receive the crown of life** that God has promised to **those who love him**.*

13 No one undergoing a trial should say, "I am being tempted by God,"
- *since God is not **tempted by evil**,*
- *and he himself **doesn't tempt anyone**. 14*
- *But **each person is tempted** when he is **drawn away** and **enticed** by **his own evil desire**. 15*

*Then after **desire** has **conceived**,*
- *it gives **birth** to **sin**,*
  - *and when **sin** is **fully grown**,*

[30] https://www.blueletterbible.org/lang/lexicon/lexicon.cfm?Strongs=G5083&t=KJV (May 19,2020)

> • *it gives* **birth** *to* **death**. "**James 1:12-15 CSB)**

So now that we have supported our premise with scripture, using the analogy of Scripture where scripture verifies or confirms scripture, we have proven the point biblically. Also notice that James tells you through endurance you receive the crown of life where was this mentioned earlier?

> "*Don't be afraid of what* **you are about to suffer**. *Look, the devil is about to throw some of you into prison to test you, and* **you will experience affliction** *for ten days.*
> * *Be faithful to the* **point of death**,
> * *and* **I will give you the crown of life**." **Revelation 2:10 (CSB)**

Scripture is clear! Yes, **saints** can experience wrath, But the wrath they experience **is not from GOD**. This wrath comes from Satan:

> "......*because* **the devil** *has come down to you*
> *with* **great fury**...", **Revelation 12:12 (CSB)**
> ".....*For* **the devil** *has come down to you, having* **great wrath**....." **Revelation 12:12(NKJV)**

WHO DOES THE BIBLE SAY THE WRATH OF GOD COMES UPON? ZEPHANIAH 1:14-18

The premise in the pre-tribulation rapture view is that we are removed so that the wrath of God doesn't Come upon God's people. We will explore the verses in context and determine from the evidence, **who God says receives His wrath**.

> "*The great day of the Lord is near, near and rapidly approaching. Listen, the day of the Lord —then the warrior's cry is bitter.* 15 **That day is a day of wrath**, *a day of* **trouble** *and* **distress**, *a day of destruction and* **desolation, a day of darkness** *and* **gloom**, *a day of* **clouds** *and* **total darkness**, 16 *a day of* **trumpet blast** *and* **battle cry against the fortified cities**, *and against the high corner towers.* 17 **I will bring distress on mankind**, *and they will walk like the blind* **because they have sinned against the Lord**. *Their blood will be poured out like dust and their flesh like dung.* 18 *Their silver and their gold will be unable to rescue them on* **the day of the Lord's wrath**. *The whole earth will be consumed by the fire of his jealousy, for he will make a complete, yes, a horrifying end of all the inhabitants of the earth.*" **Zephaniah 1:14-18 (CSB)**

This first example is simply to demonstrate Biblically that the one who **sins against God receives His wrath**.

> *"The Father loves the Son and has given all things into his hands. 36* **The one who believes in the Son has eternal life,** *but* **the one who rejects the Son will not see life;** *instead,* **the wrath of God remains on him.** *"* **John 3:35-36(CSB)**

This is easily expressed, the **unbelievers who reject receive the wrath of God**.

> *"***For God's wrath is revealed from heaven**
> - **against all godlessness and unrighteousness of people who by their unrighteousness suppress the truth,**
> *19 since what can be known about God is evident among them, because God has shown it to them. 20 For his invisible attributes, that is, his eternal power and divine nature, have been clearly seen since the creation of the world, being understood through what he has made.* **As a result, people are without excuse.** *21 For though* **they knew God,**
> - **they did not glorify him as God** *or* **show gratitude.** *Instead, their* **thinking became worthless,** *and their senseless hearts were darkened. 22*
> - *Claiming to be wise,* **they became fools** *23 and* **exchanged the glory** *of the* **immortal God** *for images* **resembling mortal man, birds, four-footed animals,** *and* **reptiles.**
> *24 Therefore* **God delivered them over** *in the* **desires** *of their* **hearts** *to* **sexual impurity,** *so that their bodies were* **degraded among themselves.** *25*
> - *They exchanged* **the truth of God for a lie,** *and* **worshiped** *and* **served** *what has been* **created instead of the Creator,** *who is praised forever. Amen.*
> *26* **For this reason God delivered** *them* **over to disgraceful passions.**
> - *Their* **women exchanged natural sexual relations** *for* **unnatural ones.** *27*
> - *The* **men** *in* **the same way** *also* **left natural relations** *with* **women** *and were inflamed in* **their lust for one another.** *Men* **committed shameless acts with men** *and received in their own persons the* **appropriate penalty of their error.**
> *28 And because* **they did not think it worthwhile to acknowledge God,** *God delivered them over to a corrupt mind so that they do what is not right. 29*
> - **They are filled with all unrighteousness, evil, greed, and wickedness.**
> - **They are full of envy, murder, quarrels, deceit,** *and* **malice.**

- *They are **gossips**, 30 **slanderers**, God-**haters**, **arrogant, proud, boastful, inventors of evil, disobedient** to **parents**, 31 **senseless, untrustworthy, unloving**, and **unmerciful**.*

*32 Although they know God's just sentence — that **those who practice such things deserve to die** —*

- *they not only **do them**, but **even applaud** others who practice them." Romans 1:18-32 (CSB)*

Surely you do not practice the things mentioned in these passages? NO, **then the wrath of God** is not for you according to scripture

1) God's wrath comes down on those in this list of offenses.
2) Please notice the target audience. The first line says that **God's wrath** is appointed to these **individuals.**

*"Therefore, **be imitators of God**, as dearly loved children, 2 and walk in love, as Christ also loved us and gave himself for us, a sacrificial and fragrant offering to God. 3 But **sexual immorality** and **any impurity** or **greed** should **not even be heard of among you**, as is proper for saints. 4 **Obscene and foolish talking** or **crude joking** are not **suitable**, but rather **giving thanks**. 5 For know and recognize this: Every **sexually immoral** or **impure** or **greedy person**, who is an **idolater**, does not have an **inheritance** in **the kingdom of Christ** and of **God**. 6 Let no one **deceive you with empty arguments**, for God's wrath is coming on the disobedient because of these things. 7 Therefore, do not become their partners. 8 **For you were once darkness, but now you are light in the Lord**. Live as children of light —" Ephesians 5:1-5 (CSB)*

Once again, notice:

1) there are certain targeted persons in each passage,
2) and there are those who are told **these things will not befall them**. And that they should walk in light. Is God taking the light out of the world? NO!

God is not punishing these in the light, God knows his targets.

*"**So if you have been raised with Christ**, seek the things above, where Christ is, seated at the right hand of God. 2 **Set your minds on things above, not on earthly things**. 3 For you died, and your life is hidden with Christ in God.*

4 When Christ, who is your life, appears, then you also will appear with him in glory.

- *5 **Therefore, put to death what belongs to your earthly nature: sexual immorality, impurity, lust, evil desire**, and **greed, which is idolatry**.*
- *6 Because of these, God's **wrath is coming upon the disobedient**,*

*7 and you **once walked** in **these things** when you **were living in them**.*

- *8 But now, put away all the following: anger, wrath, malice, slander, and **filthy language** from your mouth.*
- *9 Do not lie to one another, since you have put off the **old self with its practices***

*10 and have put on **the new self**. You are being **renewed** in **knowledge** according to **the image of your Creator**."* **Colossians 3:1-10(CSB)**

As we read the message is given **God's wrath** is on the **disobedient**.

1. Take note of the contrast about your old ways and what you are currently doing as a believer.
2. In verses 5 and 6 key points are given. These are the things to put off, in **verse** 6 the **wrath** hits those who are disobedient.
3. Do not forget the subject at hand, wrath. When the verses are read closely there is still no hint of any separation of any groups.
4. Notice verse 4 says, **when Christ who is your life appears**. The **context** is **to the church and how you will appear** with HIM in glory. This **glory** is revealed in the **resurrected saints** and **saints alive at his coming**.

Here are two examples of this

1ˢᵗ Corinthians 15:42 *"So it is with the **resurrection of the dead**: Sown in corruption, raised in incorruption; 43 sown in dishonor, **raised in glory**; sown in weakness, raised in power;"*

2ⁿᵈ Thessalonians 1:10 *"on **that day when he comes** to be **glorified by his saints** and to be marveled at **by all those who have believed**, because our testimony among you was believed. 11 In view of this, we always pray for you that our God will make you worthy of his calling, and by his power fulfill your every desire to do good and your work produced by faith, 12 so that the name of our Lord Jesus will be glorified by you, and you by him, according to the grace of our **God and the Lord Jesus Christ**."*

Observe the details in these other verses, on the subject, in the book of Revelation where the **wrath of God** is poured out, and **who are the recipients of His wrath**?

*"**Then the kings of the earth, the nobles, the generals, the rich, the powerful, and every slave and free person hid in the caves** and among the rocks of the mountains. 16 And they said to the mountains and to the rocks, "**Fall on us and hide us from the face of the one seated on the throne and from the wrath of the Lamb**, 17 because the great day of **their wrath has come**! And who is able to stand?"* **Revelation 6:15-17 (CSB)**

*"The **nations were angry**, but **your wrath has come**. The time has come for the **dead** to **be judged and to give the***

reward to your servants the prophets, to the saints, and to those who fear your name, both small and great, and the time has come to destroy those who destroy the earth. 19 Then the temple of God in heaven was opened, and the ark of his covenant appeared in his temple. There were flashes of lightning, rumblings and peals of thunder, an earthquake, and severe hail."
Revelation 11:18-19(CSB)

"And another, a second angel, followed, saying, "It has fallen, Babylon the Great has fallen. She made all the nations drink the wine of her sexual immorality, which brings wrath." 9 And another, a third angel, followed them and spoke with a loud voice: "If anyone worships the beast and its image and receives a mark on his forehead or on his hand, 10 he will also drink the wine of God's wrath, which is poured full strength into the cup of his anger. He will be tormented with fire and sulfur in the sight of the holy angels and in the sight of the Lamb, 11 and the smoke of their torment will go up forever and ever. There is no rest day or night for those who worship the beast and its image, or anyone who receives the mark of its name.

- *12 This calls for endurance from the saints, who keep God's commands and their faith in Jesus."*
Revelation 14:8-12 (CSB)

The evidence has shown without contradiction who the **wrath** is coming on.

But **the saints**
- endure
- and go through this time
- and are not taken out!

THE QUESTION OF TRIBULATION SAINTS

If anyone says to you these are **tribulation saints,** please ask them to show you this contextually. They must be able to demonstrate, contextually,
- that this particular group of unbelievers became believers (a part from all other believers)
- and that this group of saints were the only group of saints ever instructed to endure to the end,
- and that the Scripture addresses only this group of Saints only as the tribulation saints.
- And where in all the Scripture does the Bible split Saints up into Old Testament, New Testament, and Tribulation saints?

Ask them to demonstrate it with Scripture: **Giving the verses that support their premise.**

The popular web site, Got Questions[31], says that the Two Witnesses will preach the Gospel to the so-called **Tribulation Saints**. For this to be true, the *Two Witnesses* would have to be on the earth during the Great Tribulation, also known as the last three and a half years.

> The article: "The tribulation saints will hear the gospel from several possible sources. The first is the Bible; there will be many copies of the Bible left in the world, and when God's judgments begin to fall, many people will likely react by finding a Bible to see if prophecies are being fulfilled. Many of the tribulation saints will also have heard the gospel from the two witnesses (Revelation 11:1–13). The Bible says these two individuals "will prophesy for 1,260 days [three and a half years]" (verse 3) and perform great miracles (verse 6). And then there are the 144,000 Jewish missionaries who are redeemed and sealed by God during the tribulation (Revelation 7:1–8). Immediately following the description of their sealing in Revelation 7, we read of the multitudes of tribulation saints who are saved from every corner of the world (verses 9–17)."

Questions, one should ask "Got-Questions based on their assertions with a Bible in-hand:"
1. When does the Two Witnesses ministry end?
2. Will the Two Witnesses be preaching to the Tribulation saints?
3. Will the 144,00 from the nation of Israel be preaching to the Tribulation saints?

The Scripture is clear as to when the Two Witnesses ministry began and when it ended. We can verify as to whether the assertion by Got Questions is accurate about the Two Witnesses preaching the gospel to Tribulation Saints.

Now their ministry starts in Revelation 11:3 where it says they were given the power to prophesy one thousand two hundred and threescore days.
- When we do the math, we know that their ministry is only three and a half years.

> "But **after** three and a half days, the breath of life from God entered them, and they stood on their feet. Great fear fell on those who saw them. 12 Then they heard a loud voice from heaven saying to them, "Come up here."
> - **They went up to heaven in a cloud**, while their enemies watched them. 13

---

31 https://www.gotquestions.org/tribulation-saints.html (November 18, 2020)

- *13 **At that moment a violent earthquake took place,***

a tenth of the city fell, and seven thousand people were killed in the earthquake. The survivors were terrified and gave glory to the God of heaven." **Revelation 11:11-13 (CSB)**

According to Revelation 11:13 in the same moment a Great earthquake happens these Two witnesses go up into heaven.

Notice, as this is happening the remnant is escaping from the great flood of men who are chasing them, where do we find this? Revelation chapter 12:

"The woman was given two wings of a great eagle, so that she could fly from the serpent's presence to her place in the wilderness, where she was nourished for
- ***a time, times, and half a time.***

15 From his mouth the serpent spewed
- ***water** like a river flowing after the woman, to sweep her away with **a flood.** 16*
- *But **the earth** helped the woman. **The earth opened its mouth** and swallowed up the river*

*that the dragon had spewed from his mouth." **Revelation 12:14-16 (CSB)***

The Woman (Israel) is fleeing into her safe place for **three and a half years** (v.14). The earth is opened (earthquake) and swallows up the flood which *is a **symbol of an army** (people)*. In conclusion, The Two witnesses die at the very beginning (of the latter 3 ½ years) which is The Great Tribulation. There is no way the Two Witnesses can be preaching the gospel to the So-called Tribulation Saints as defined by pre-tribulationist after they have died and risen and gone into heaven.

It is evident in Scriptures that the 144,000 are sealed by the servants of God during the beginning of the Great Tribulation (3 ½ years into the 7-year tribulation).

Based on the assertions of "Got Questions", does the Bible support the assertion that this group, 144,000, will be preaching the Gospel to the Tribulation Saints.

The Scriptures tell us in the book:
- Revelation 6:16-17 The Great Day of God's wrath has begun.
- Revelation 7:1-4 the angels are told to seal the 144,000 on their foreheads so they are not harmed.

But there is no evidence presented showing this group, the 144,000, evangelizing to anyone, during the last half of the seven years of tribulation.

- The next big event with the 144,000 is found in Revelation 14:1 where they are standing with the Lord on Mt Sion.
- A similar account happens in Ezekiel 9:1-11 when God was punishing Israel and Judah for their iniquity.

> "and the Lord said to him, "Go through the midst of the city, through the midst of Jerusalem, **and put a mark on the foreheads of the men** who sigh and cry over all the abominations that are done within it."" **Ezekiel 9:4 (NKJV)**

- In fact, the reason these witnesses, 144,000, are given this seal is so that when the locusts are released from the bottomless pit they won't be killed. We find this in Revelation chapter 9:

> "They were commanded not to harm the grass of the earth, or any green thing, or any tree, but only those men who do not have the seal of God on their foreheads." **Revelation 9:4 (NKJV)**

No, Scriptures verify that the 144,000 is preaching during the Great Tribulation. In conclusion, we see the wrath of God is on the earth and the Scripture demonstrates only the church and the angels preaching the Gospel (Revelation 14:6).

"Then **another angel** who also had a **sharp sickle** came out of the **temple in heaven.** 18 **Yet another angel**, who had authority over fire, **came from the altar**, and he called with a loud voice to the one who had the sharp sickle, "Use your sharp sickle and gather the clusters of grapes from the **vineyard of the earth**, because its grapes have ripened." 19 **So the angel** swung his sickle **at the earth** and gathered the **grapes from the vineyard of the earth**, and he **threw them** into the great winepress of **God's wrath.** 20 Then the press was trampled outside the city, and blood flowed out of the press up to the horses' bridles for about 180 miles." **Revelation 14:17-20 (CSB)**

Now as we see the **wrath of GOD** being poured out on **unbelievers.** Notice it is only angels doing the work, always paying attention to the details that God leaves us.

"Then I heard a loud voice from the temple saying to the seven angels, **"Go and pour out the seven bowls of God's wrath on the earth."** 2 The first went and poured out his bowl on the earth, **and severely painful sores broke out on the people who had the mark of the beast and who worshiped his image.** 3 The second poured out his bowl into the sea. It turned to blood like that of a dead person, and all life in the sea died. 4 The third poured out his bowl into the rivers and the springs of water, and they became blood. 5 I heard the angel of the waters say, You are just, the Holy One, who is and who was, because you have passed judgment on these things. 6 **Because they poured out the blood of the saints and the prophets**, you have given them blood to drink; **they deserve it!** 7 I heard the altar say, Yes, Lord God, the Almighty, **true and just are your judgments**. 8 The fourth poured out his bowl on the sun. It was allowed to scorch people with fire, 9 and people were scorched by the intense heat. **So they blasphemed the name of God**, who has the power over these plagues, **and they did not repent and give him glory**. 10 The fifth poured out his bowl **on the throne of the beast, and its kingdom** was plunged into darkness. **People gnawed their tongues because of their pain** 11 **and blasphemed the God of heaven because of their pains and their sores**, but they **did not repent** of their works. 12 The sixth poured out his bowl on the great river Euphrates, and its water was dried up to prepare the way for the kings from the east. 13 Then I saw three unclean spirits like frogs coming from the **dragon's mouth, from the beast's mouth**, and **from** the **mouth of the false prophet**. 14 For they are demonic spirits performing signs, **who travel to the kings of the whole world to assemble them** for the battle on the great day of God, the Almighty. 15 "Look, I am coming like a thief. **Blessed is the one who is alert and remains clothed** so that he may not go around naked and people see his shame." 16 So they assembled the kings at the place called in Hebrew, Armageddon. 17 Then the seventh poured out his bowl into the air, and a loud voice came out of the temple from the throne, saying, "It is done!" 18 There were flashes of lightning, rumblings, and peals of thunder. And a severe earthquake occurred like no other since people have been on the earth, so great was the quake. 19 The great city split into three parts, and the cities of the nations fell. **Babylon the Great was remembered in God's presence**; he gave her the **cup filled with the wine of his fierce anger**." **Revelation 16:1-19 (CSB)**

Pay attention to all the **participants** who **received God's wrath** in this chapter. It strikes rite at the heart of the argument of **who receives God's wrath and who does not**.

"After this I saw **another angel** with great authority coming down **from heaven**, and the earth was illuminated by his splendor. 2 He called out in a mighty voice: It has fallen, **Babylon the Great** has fallen! **She has become** a **home** for **demons**, a haunt for **every unclean spirit**, a haunt for **every unclean bird**, and a haunt for **every unclean** and **despicable beast**. 3 For **all the nations have drunk the wine** of her sexual immorality, **which brings wrath**. The **kings of the earth** have **committed sexual immorality with her**, and the **merchants of the earth** have grown wealthy from her sensuality and excess. 4 Then I heard another voice from heaven: **Come out of her, my people**, so that you **will not share** in **her sins** or receive any **of her plagues**. 5

*For her sins are piled up to heaven, and **God has remembered her crimes.** "* **Revelation 18:1-5 (CSB)**

The Church of Thyatira is warned to come out of Mystery Babylon and have no parts of her wickedness this is also addressed in Revelation Chapter 18. If the Church is told by the Lord to come from amongst this wicked system, how is it that teachers and scholars teach that the church has been removed in a pre-tribulation rapture?

At this point it has **thoroughly been shown who the word of God says the wrath comes upon**, and that true believers will be on the earth going through and will **not be targeted by God** to receive that which falls on **unbelievers**.

CHAPTER EIGHT

THE PRE-TRIBULATION:

The pre-tribulation view says that the Church is not mentioned between chapter 4 and 18 because it has been raptured. With that in mind, let us take a closer look at this, and the evidence of the book itself.

One of the major problems I see with this argument is that, if one says the Church (the servants of God) is gone (removed), then it makes God look illogical.

I find it quite strange that God gives this revelation to John and he clearly tells who He is writing to (seven Churches of Asia minor), **here is the illogical part if God is writing to a Church** that **is raptured** before the events happen.

> Why did God write to the Church, did He not know that it would be gone? or did he just want it to be a mystery?

So, the book of Revelation chapter one starts off like many of the New Testament books it gives you an **introduction of whom it is written to**, and a closing. Let's see how this plays out in the Scriptures.

> *"The revelation of Jesus Christ that God gave him to show*
> - ***his servants what must soon take place.***
> - *He made it known by sending his angel to **his servant** John,*
>
> *2 who testified to **the word of God and to the testimony of Jesus Christ**, whatever he saw. 3*
> - ***Blessed is the one who reads aloud** the **words of this prophecy,***
> - *and **blessed are those who hear the words of this prophecy***
>   - ○ *and **keep what is written in it,***
>
> ***because the time is near.***
> *4 John:*
> - ***To the seven churches** in Asia.*
>
> *Grace and peace to you from the **one who is, who was, and who is to come,** and from the seven spirits before his throne, 5 and from Jesus Christ, the faithful witness, the firstborn from the dead and the ruler of the kings of the earth. To him who loves us **and has set us free from our sins by his blood,** 6 and made us a kingdom, priests to his God and Father — to him be glory and dominion forever and ever. Amen."* **Revelation 1:1-6 (CSB)**

Now that we see who the passages are **addressed to, (His servants, His Churches),** (verse 1,4), let's connect these verses with what we see in the

The Pre-tribulation:

book of Revelation to support our argument that the **church is here during The Great Tribulation**.

The church in Thyatira:
"But I have this against you:

- **You tolerate the woman Jezebel**, *who calls herself a prophetess*
    - *and* **teaches and deceives my servants to commit sexual immorality** *and to eat meat sacrificed to idols.*

21 I gave her time to **repent**,

- *but she does not want to* **repent** *of her sexual immorality.* *22 Look, I* **will throw her into a sickbed and those who commit adultery with her into great affliction**.
    - *Unless they repent of her works, 23 I will strike her children dead.*
        - **Then all the churches will know that I am the one who examines minds and hearts, and I will give to each of you according to your works**.*"* **Revelation 2:20-23 (CSB)**

If she can be found in the **Great tribulation** period, Who is this woman Jezebel? vs 20 Known as the Harlot, if she can be found during the Great Tribulation which is known as the latter half of the Seven-year Tribulation, then:

1. the view that the Church has been raptured is disproven.
2. and the **Church** (servants) **must be there to be seduced by her.**

Notice:

"When he opened the fifth seal, I saw under the altar the souls of those who had been slaughtered because of the word of God and the testimony they had given. 10 They cried out with a loud voice: "Lord, the one who is holy and true, how long until you judge those who live on the earth and avenge our blood? " 11 So they were each given a white robe, and they were told to rest a little while longer until the number would be completed of their ***fellow servants and their brothers and sisters***, *who were going to be killed just as they had been."* **Revelation 6:9-11 (CSB)**

Furthermore, When the fifth seal is opened, God instructs them to rest until the rest of their brothers are killed as they were. If the Scripture calls believers on the earth brothers, then the implication Is that they are members of the *Body of Christ* which is the Church.

Immediately after the sixth seal is opened:

"And they said to the mountains and to the rocks, "Fall on us and hide us from the face of the one seated on the throne and ***from the wrath***

The Pre-tribulation:

> *of the Lamb, 17 because the great day of **their wrath has come!**
> And who is able to stand?"* **Revelation 6:16-17 (CSB)**

Scripture informed us that the wrath of God is upon the earth and is taking place; notice this starts in Revelation chapter 6 verses 16-17. As we conclude, we understand that the Church is present during The Great Tribulation, But the Church is not hiding from The Lamb and the Wrath of God.

> *"Then one of the seven angels who had the seven bowls came and spoke with me: "Come, I will show you the judgment of the*
> - ***Notoriously Prostitute*** *who is seated on **many waters**.*
> *2 The kings of the earth a **sexual immorality with her, and those who live on the earth became drunk on the wine of her sexual immorality**." 3 Then he carried me away in the Spirit to a wilderness.*
> - *I **saw** a **woman sitting** on a **scarlet beast** that was covered with blasphemous names and had seven heads and ten horns.*
> *4 **The woman** was dressed in purple and scarlet, adorned with gold, jewels, and pearls. **She** had a golden cup in **her** hand filled **with everything detestable** and with **the impurities of her prostitution**.*
> *5 On her forehead was written a name, a **mystery: Babylon** the Great, the **Mother of prostitutes** and of the **detestable Things of the earth**. 6 Then*
> - *I saw that **the woman was drunk with the blood of the saints** and **with the blood of the witnesses to Jesus**.*
> *When I saw her, I was greatly astonished."* **Revelation 17:1-6 (CSB)**

Now after reading those two passages there should be no doubt that the Church itself is present during **The Great Tribulation**. But of course, there are some who still do not believe. Here are some other facts to consider supporting our argument.

Whose blood is **the woman** drunk with**? SAINTS.**

> *"After this I saw another angel with great authority coming down from heaven, and the earth was illuminated by his splendor. 2 He called out in a mighty voice:*
> - ***It has fallen, Babylon the Great has fallen!***
> - ***She** has become a home for demons, a haunt for every unclean spirit, a haunt for every unclean bird, and a haunt for every unclean and despicable beast.*
> *3 **For all the nations have drunk the wine of her sexual immorality**, which **brings wrath**. The kings of the earth have*

The Pre-tribulation:

> *committed sexual immorality with her, and the merchants of the*
> *earth have grown wealthy from her sensuality and excess.* 4
> - *Then I heard another **voice from heaven**: Come out of*
>   ***her, my people,***
> ***so that you will not share in her sins or receive any of her***
> ***plagues."*** **Revelation 18:1-4 (CSB)**

It is very clear in light of the passages starting In Revelation chapter two that God **addressed the Church** and told her to repent and turn back to Him or they would receive **His wrath**, so how can anyone tell you the Church isn't present when the **Scriptures plainly show that they are addressed and warned** (*v.4*), until the very end of this system.

Revelation 19:1-7 was covered in detail,
After this I heard something like the loud voice of a **vast multitude** in heaven, saying, Hallelujah! Salvation, glory, and power belong to our God, **because his judgments are true and righteous**, because

- he has **judged the notorious prostitute** who corrupted the earth with her sexual immorality.
  - ○ **and he has avenged the blood of his servants that was on her hands** (*v. 2*).
  - ○ A voice came from the throne, saying, praise our God, **all his servants**, and the ones who fear him, both small and great (*v. 5*)!
- Then I heard something like the voice of a vast multitude, like the sound of cascading waters, and like the rumbling of loud thunder, saying, Hallelujah, **because our Lord God, the Almighty, reigns** (*v. 6*)!
- Let us be glad, rejoice, and give him glory, **because the marriage of the Lamb has come**, and his bride has prepared herself (*v. 7*).

Question in the passage, above, **how did** the harlot get **the blood** of God's servants (***the Church***) on Her hands (v. 6), if they were raptured? This simply could not have happened.

Who Is telling Bible believers the truth? The scholars or the text? Of course, the answer should be, the text.

JESUS tells **His Church** to continue **until He comes.** The Scripture in context clearly teaches that Jesus does not return until the end of tribulation.

> *"I **say** to the **rest of you in Thyatira**, who do not hold this*
> *teaching, who haven't known "the so-called secrets of Satan" — as*
> *they say — I am not putting any other burden on you. 25 **Only***
> ***hold on to what you have until I come.** 26 The one **who***

> ***conquers and*** *who **keeps my works to the end***: *I will give him authority over the nations —"* **Revelation 2:24-26 (CSB)**

G3528 nikao[32] **the one who overcomes** – for the Christian, is the one that holds fast their faith **even unto the death** against the power of their foes, and **temptations** and **persecutions**.

Outline of Biblical Usage G3528:

I.   to conquer
  A. to carry off the victory, come off victorious
      i.   of Christ, victorious over all His foes
      ii.   of Christians, that hold fast their faith even unto death against the power of their foes, and temptations and persecutions
      iii. when one is arraigned or goes to law, to win the case, maintain one's cause

Examples of those who lost their lives. These were victorious because they overcame Satan by holding fast their faith:

- *"He who has an ear, let him hear what the Spirit says to the churches. He who overcomes shall not be hurt by the second death."* **Revelation 2:11 (NKJV)**
- *"To him who overcomes I will grant to sit with Me on My throne, as I also overcame and sat down with My Father on His throne."* **Revelation 3:21 (NKJV)**
- "And they overcame him by the blood of the Lamb and by the word of their testimony, and they did not love their lives to the death.' **Revelation 12:11 (NKJV)**

Examples of those who were overcome by others:

- *"When they finish their testimony, the beast that ascends out of the bottomless pit will make war against them, overcome them, and kill them."* **Revelation 11:7 (NKJV)**
- *"It was granted to him to make war with the saints and to overcome them. And authority was given him over every tribe, tongue, and nation.* **Revelation 13:7 (NKJV)**
- *"These will make war with the Lamb, and the Lamb will overcome them, for He is Lord of lords and King of kings; and those who are with Him are called, chosen, and faithful."* **Revelation 17:14 (NKJV)**

Allowing the scripture to interpret scripture, we see that the Church is mentioned, and there are instructions to the Church:

---

[32] https://www.blueletterbible.org/lang/lexicon/lexicon.cfm?Strongs=G3528&t=KJV

The Pre-tribulation:

The church in Sardis:
'"Write to the angel   of the **church** in **Sardis**: Thus says the one who has the seven spirits of God and the seven stars: I know your works; you have a reputation for being alive, but you are dead. 2
- **Be alert** and strengthen what remains, which is about to die, for I have not found your works complete before my God. 3
- **Remember**, then, what you have received and heard; **keep it**, **and repent**. If you are not alert, I **will come like** a **thief, and you have no idea at what hour** I **will come upon you**.

4 But you have a few people in Sardis who have not **defiled their clothes**, and
- **they will walk with me in white**, because they **are worthy**. "In the same way, 5
- **the one who conquers** will be dressed in white clothes, and I will never erase his name from the book of life but will acknowledge his name before my Father and before his angels.

6 "**Let anyone who has ears to hear listen**   to what the **Spirit says to the churches**."' **Revelation 3:1-6 (CSB)**

Let us see if those mentioned in the **church of Sardis** that walk with Christ in white who overcomes until the death.

"When he opened the fifth seal, I saw under the altar **the souls** of those who had been **slaughtered** because of **the word of God and the testimony they had given**. 10 They cried out with a loud voice, "Lord, the one who is holy and true, how long until you judge those who live on the earth and **avenge our blood**?" 11 So they were each given a **white robe**, and they were told to **rest** a **little while longer** until the **number would be completed** of their **fellow servants** and their **brothers and sisters**, who were going **to be killed just as they had been**." **Revelation 6:9-11 (CSB)**

Most definitely the **Church** was addressed and given **warning** and told what it **would receive** if it (the Saints) **overcame** the **persecutions** which were **before** the Church, and we can see that it is **mentioned** throughout **chapters 4-18** in the **book of Revelation**.

The Church in Philadelphia:
'"Write to the angel of the **Church** in Philadelphia: Thus says the Holy One, the true one, the one who has the key of David, **who opens and no one will close**, **and who closes and no one opens**: 8 I know your works. Look, I have placed before you an **open door** that no one can close because you have but little power; yet you have kept my word and have not denied my name. 9 Note this: I will make those from the synagogue of Satan, who claim to be Jews and are not, but are lying — I will make them

The Pre-tribulation:

> come and bow down at your feet, and they will know that I have
> loved you. 10 **Because you have kept my command to
> endure**, I will also **keep you from the hour of testing** that is
> going to come on the whole world to **test those** who live on the
> earth. 11 I **am coming soon**. Hold on to what you have, **so that
> no one takes your crown.** 12 "The one **who conquers** I **will
> make** a **pillar** in the **temple of my God**, and he will never go
> out again. I **will write on him** the **name of my God** and the
> name of the city of my God — **the new Jerusalem**, which
> **comes down out of heaven** from my God — and my **new
> name**."' **Revelation 3:7-12 (CSB)**

Where can we see these things happening that are promised in the above
verses.

> "Then he said to me, "These words are faithful and true. The Lord,
> the God of the spirits of the prophets, has sent his angel to show
> his **servants what must soon take place**." "Look, I am
> coming soon! **Blessed is the one who keeps the words of
> the prophecy of this book**." I, John, am the one who heard and
> saw these things. When I heard and saw them, I fell down to
> worship at the feet of the angel who had shown them to me. But
> he said to me, "**Don't do that**! I **am** a **fellow servant** with you,
> your brothers the prophets, **and those who keep the words of
> this book. Worship God!**" Then he said to me, "Don't seal up
> the words of the prophecy of this book, because the time is near.
> Let the unrighteous go on in unrighteousness; let the filthy still be
> filthy; **let the righteous** go on in **righteousness**; let the **holy**
> still be **holy**." "Look, I **am coming soon, and my reward is
> with me to repay each person according to his work**. I am
> the Alpha and the Omega, the first and the last, the beginning and
> the end. "**Blessed** are those who **wash their robes**, so that they
> may have the right to the **tree of life** and may enter the city by
> the gates. Outside are the dogs, the sorcerers, the sexually
> immoral, the murderers, the idolaters, and everyone who loves
> and practices falsehood. "I, **Jesus, have sent my angel to
> attest these things to you for the churches**. I am the Root
> and descendant of David, the bright morning star." Both the Spirit
> and the bride say, "Come!" **Let anyone who hears, say,
> "Come!"** Let the one who is **thirsty come**. Let the one who
> desires take the **water of life freely**. **Revelation 22:6-17 (CBS)**

The closing of the book of Revelation chapter 22 summed up
all things that were instructed of Jesus and given to John to
reveal to the Church:

1. **blessed is he who keeps the words of the prophecy
of this book.**

2. **keep your garments clean, stay righteous until the Messiah comes.**

Now if these are the instructions to the Church, how can anyone conclude that the Church is raptured away before The Great Tribulation?

CHAPTER NINE

THE IMMINENT RETURN OF CHRIST

From the pre-tribulation adherent's point of view, the imminent return of Christ is described as a sudden return on any given day. Since this is the argument that is put before us, it is our duty to do what Acts 17:11 says; and make sure that the evidence which we received is accurate according to the authorities which came before us.

CHRIST MAY RETURN AT ANY TIME

> Christ return is imminent. Since Christ may return at any time, in the pre-tribulation view they take this statement to mean Christ can return at any hour like an unexpected thief that could pop up at your door.
> Let's use contextual criticism and find out.

> "*For the grace of God has appeared, bringing salvation for all people, 12 instructing us to deny godlessness and worldly lusts and to live in a sensible, righteous, and godly way in the present age, 13* **while we wait for the blessed hope, the appearing of the glory of our great God and Savior, Jesus Christ**. *14 He gave himself for us to redeem us from all lawlessness and to cleanse for himself a people for his own possession, eager to do good works.15 Proclaim these things; encourage and rebuke with all authority. Let no one disregard you.* "Titus **2:11 (CSB)**

Saints, where in this passage does it imply that Christ may return at any moment? To take the statement (v.13) **while we wait for the blessed hope** and then change the terminology of the passage to mean "<u>*Christ's return is imminent and can happen at any hour of any day*</u>" would be to insert one's own presupposition and bias to the Scripture. The text when read in its entirety is describing how a believer should walk and operate in doctrine until the Second Coming of Christ.

Our blessed hope is that **He is going to return**.

Matthew 24:42-44 is also a verse of Scripture used to support a false premise that Jesus can return **any day**; *By saying you do not know when a thief will come.* Let us use

contextual criticism and see if this false premise is supported by the text.

> "*Therefore be alert, since you don't know* **what day** *your Lord is coming. 43 But know this: If the homeowner had known what time the thief was coming, he would have stayed alert and not let his house be broken into. 44 This is why you are also to be ready, because the Son of Man is coming at* **an hour** *you do not expect.*"
> **Matthew 24:42-44 (CSB)**

Note: *contextual criticism is a simple analysis of the detailed information given in a written text.*

The context of Matthew 24 is that there is a continuous plea "**to watch and be prepared**". The passages are not evidence of an Imminent Return where the Messiah could return at **any given day**. This would not only change the context, but it would also change the definition of (**What day**) to mean immediately or any day.

Even so the Church should be constantly watching for **the signs** and preparing themselves.

The Scripture backs up our premise that Saints will be watching until His return and that it will be well with them regardless of whether they are alive or departed. Saints are commanded to be faithful and to endured even to the point of death.

Where should we go?

> '" ***About the times and the seasons***: *Brothers and sisters, you do not need anything to be written to you.*
> *2 For you yourselves know very well that*
> - **the day of the Lord** *will come* **just like a thief in the night**. *3*
>
> *When* **they** *say,* "**Peace and security**,"
> - **then sudden destruction will come upon them**, *like labor pains on a pregnant woman,*
> - *and* **they will not escape**. *4*
>
> *But you, brothers and sisters,*
> - **are not in the dark**, *for this day to surprise you like a thief. 5*
> - **For you are all**
>   - *children* **of light** *and*
>   - *children* **of the day**.
> - *We do not belong to the night or the darkness. 6*
>
> *So then,* **let us not sleep**,
> - *like the rest,*
> - *but* **let us stay awake** *and be self-controlled.*

7 *For those*
- *who sleep, sleep at night,*

and those
- *who get drunk, get drunk at night.*

*8 But since **we belong to the day**,*
- *let us be self-controlled*
- *and put on the armor of faith and love,*
- *and a helmet of the hope of salvation.*

*9 **For God did not appoint us to wrath**, but to obtain **salvation** through **our Lord Jesus Christ**, 10 who died for us, so that whether*
- *we are **awake** or **asleep**,*
  we may live together with him. 11 Therefore encourage one another and build each other up as you are already doing.'" 1st **Thessalonians 5:1-11(CSB)**

So contextually these verses show that the Church will be here on earth when CHRIST returns keeping watch with their full armor on waiting for rewards not worrying whether **they are alive or dead**. Because their ultimate salvation Is in THE LORD. Jesus says the very same thing to His disciples in **Matthew 24:43-44 (CSB):**

*"'But know this: If the homeowner had known what time the thief was coming, **he would have stayed alert** and not let his house be broken into. 44 This is why you are also **to be ready**, because **the Son of Man is coming** at an hour you do not expect. "'*

The return of Christ is assured that doesn't mean we should add to the text that which is not written or sound to doctrine. Our job is to be on alert for His return so that we don't stray. "Now concerning that day or hour no one knows — neither the angels in heaven nor the Son — but only the Father.

*"**Watch! Be alert!** For you don't know when the time is coming. 34 "It is like a man on a journey, who left his house, gave authority to his servants, gave each one his work, and commanded the doorkeeper to be alert. 35 **Therefore be alert**, since you don't know when the master of the house is coming — whether in the evening or at midnight or at the crowing of the rooster or early in the morning. 36 Otherwise,*
- *when **he comes** suddenly*
- *he might find **you sleeping**.*

*37 And what I say to you, I say to everyone: **Be alert!**"* **Mark 13:33 (CSB)**

Where In the context does it tell us that He can come on any day **before** the signs of His coming?

Brothers and sisters that would contradict what Christ himself said and the signs he gave His followers to watch for. The main point is to be prepared to receive Him at His return. Even so, one's soul could be required any moment, instantly (Luke 12:29; Acts 5:5,10).

Where should we look to find what Christ said?

"While he was sitting on the Mount of Olives, the disciples approached **him privately** and said, "**Tell us**,
- when will these things happen?
- And what is the sign of your coming
- and of the end of the age?" 4

Jesus replied to them:
- "Watch out that **no one deceives you**. 5
- For many will come in my name, saying, 'I am the Messiah,' and they will deceive many. 6
- You are going to hear of wars and rumors of wars.

See that you are not alarmed, because these things must take place, **but the end is not yet**. 7
- For nation will rise up against nation, and kingdom against kingdom.
- There will be famines and earthquakes in various places. 8

All these events are the beginning of labor pains.

9 "Then they will hand you over to be persecuted,
- and they will kill you.
- **You will be** hated by all nations because of **my name**. 10
- **Then many** will fall away, betray one another, and hate one another. 11
- **Many** false prophets will rise up and deceive many. 12 Because lawlessness will multiply, the love of many will grow cold. 13

But the one who endures to the end will be saved. 14
- This good news of the kingdom **will be** proclaimed in all the world **as a testimony** to all nations,

and **then the end will come**.

15 "**So when you see** the abomination of desolation, spoken of by the prophet Daniel, standing in the holy place" (let the reader understand), 16 "**then those in Judea must flee** to the mountains. 17
- A man on the housetop **must not** come down to get things out of his house, 18
- and a man in the field **must not** go back to get his coat. 19

- **Woe to** pregnant women and nursing **mothers in those days**! 20
- **Pray that your** escape **may not be** in winter or on a Sabbath.

21 For at that time **there will be great distress**, the kind that **hasn't taken place** from the beginning of the world until now and never will again.

22 Unless those days were cut short, **no one would be saved**. But those days will be cut short because of the elect.

23 "If anyone tells you then, '**See, here is the Messiah!**' or, 'Over here!' **do not believe it**. 24

- For false messiahs and false prophets **will arise** and **perform great signs** and wonders to lead astray, if possible, even the elect.

25 **Take note**:

- **I have told you in advance**. 26
  - So **if they tell you**,
    - 'See, he's in the wilderness!' **don't go out**; or,
    - 'See, he's in the storerooms!' **do not believe it**.
- 27 For as the lightning comes from the east and flashes as far as the west, **so will be the coming of the Son of Man**.'" **Matthew24:3-27**

CHRIST RETURN IS IMMINENT:

We know that **Christ's return is imminent, or impending** but does this mean He can return **any day** or at **any given hour**?

Scripture provides us with the evidence that **we don't know the day or the hour** and not that Jesus could return any day or any hour. There is a clear distinction.

How many times does the Bible say Jesus will return? Below are several verses used to support the faulty premise that Jesus could return at *any time*.
Please read these in the written context:

- *"Now concerning **that day and hour no one knows** — neither the angels of heaven nor the Son — except the Father alone."* **Matthew 24:36 (CSB)**
- *"Therefore be alert, because **you don't know either the day or the hour**. **Matthew 25:13 (CSB)**
- *"Now concerning **that day or hour no one knows** — neither the angels in heaven nor the Son — but only the Father."* **Mark 13:32 (CSB)**

- *"For you yourselves know very well **that the day of the Lord will come just like a thief in the night**."*
  1 Thessalonians 5:2 (CSB)

Notice the contrast between **ANY Day and Any Hour** verses *we do not know the day or the hour:*

Jesus taught, as well as Paul, that we will not see Him "*unless we see the antichrist first*". Based on their teaching, if Christ can return "at any hour" and "on any given day" that would contradict the word of God.

Let's examine the evidence, Matthew 24:15-30 you be the judge:

"'So **when you see** the abomination of desolation, spoken of by the prophet Daniel, standing in the holy place" (let the reader understand),' **Matthew 24:15 (CSB)**

Point one: Christ taught His early disciples that they would see the anti-Christ; who changed the narrative?

"For at that time there will **be great distress**, the kind that hasn't taken place from the beginning of the world until now and never will again. 22 Unless those days were cut short, no one would be saved. But those days will be cut short because of the elect." **Matthew 24:21-22 (CSB)**

Point two: Christ gave His disciples direct revelation of what would occur during the Great Tribulation (21-28).

"Immediately **after the distress** of those days, the sun will be darkened, and the moon will not shed its light; the stars will fall from the sky, and the powers of the heavens will be shaken. 30 **Then the sign** of the Son of Man will appear in the sky, and then all the peoples of the earth will mourn; and they will see the Son of Man coming on the clouds of heaven with power and great glory." **Matthew 24:29-30 (CSB)**

Point three: Christ taught that we would see Him after the distress (tribulation) of the world; And He gave His disciples **the signs** of His return. Although Jesus did not provide a day or an hour of His return, He most definitely gave us Biblical Signs that point to His return.

Paul gave the Church the same message that Jesus taught:

> *"Now concerning the coming of our Lord Jesus Christ and our being gathered to him: We ask you, brothers and sisters, 2 not to be easily upset or troubled, either by a prophecy or by a message or by a letter supposedly from us, alleging that the day of the Lord has come. [see Matthew 24:23-26]"*
> **2 Thessalonians 2:1-2 (CSB)**

Point four: Jesus and Paul both warned that we should watch and beware of those who would give false prophecy as related to His return.

> *"Don't let anyone deceive you in any way. For that day* ***will not come unless***
> • *the apostasy comes first*
> • *and the man of lawlessness is revealed, the man doomed to destruction.*
> *4 He opposes and exalts himself above every so-called god or object of worship,* ***so that he sits*** *in God's temple, proclaiming that he himself is God."* **2 Thessalonians 2:3-4 (CSB)**

Point five, six, seven: Paul concludes that the church **will not see** the Day of the Lord until

1. The apostasy happens,
2. The man of lawlessness (anti-Christ) is revealed,
3. And he sits in the temple of God.

Paul gives the same message that you will see the man of perdition before you see the Messiah.

There is no way that in Paul's epistle 1st Thessalonians 4:13-18 that he is telling you that Jesus is **returning** any day or any hour in the clouds.

> *"Then we who are still alive, who are left, will be caught up together with them in* ***the clouds*** *to meet the Lord in the air, and so we will always be with the Lord."* **1 Thessalonians 4:17 (CSB)**

Let us look at the term "**imply**":
imply- to strongly suggest the truth or existence of (something not expressly stated).

There is not a verse that states that Jesus could come back any day there is only the implication by those who add to the text and violate Proverb 30;6, Deuteronomy 4;2, Revelation 22;18 which all tell you not to add to the Word Of God.

According to Ron Rhodes' definition:

> "The term "imminent" literally means "ready to take place" or "impending." The New Testament teaches that the rapture is imminent—that is, **nothing must be fulfilled before the rapture occurs** (see 1 Corinthians 1:7; 16:22; Philippians 3:20; 4:5; 1 Thessalonians 1:10; Titus 2:13; Hebrews 9:28; James 5:7-9; 1 Peter 1:13; Jude 21). The rapture is a signless event that can occur at any moment. This is in contrast to the second coming of Christ, which is preceded by many events in the seven-year tribulation period (see Revelation 4-18)."[33]

Ron Rhodes has stated that nothing must take place before the rapture, but this book will prove that the second coming happens before the rapture.

Clearly, the Bible describes a **singular imminent return**.

Various scriptures guide us in understanding the pre-determine outcome.

> "*While he was sitting on the Mount of Olives, the disciples approached him privately and said, "**Tell us**, when will these things happen? **And what is the sign of your coming** and of the end of the age?*" **Matthew 24:3 (CSB)**

> "*For as the lightning comes from the east and flashes as far as the west, **so will be the coming** of the Son of Man.*" **Matthew 24:27 (CSB)**

> "*As the days of Noah were, **so the coming** of the Son of Man will be.*" **Matthew 24:37 (CSB)**

> "*They didn't know until the flood came and swept them all away. **This is the way the coming of the Son of Man will be.***" **Matthew 24:39 (CSB))**

> "so that you do not lack any spiritual gift as you eagerly wait for **the revelation of our Lord Jesus Christ.**" **1ˢᵗ Corinthians 1:7 (CSB)**

> "*May he make your hearts blameless in holiness before our God and Father **at the coming of our Lord Jesus** with all his saints. Amen.*" **1ˢᵗ Thessalonians 3:13 (CSB)**

---

[33] Ron Rhodes, Bible Prophecy Answer Book, Harvest House Publishers, 2017, p114

*"For we say this to you by a word from the Lord: We who are **still alive at the Lord's coming** will certainly not precede those who have fallen asleep."* **1st Thessalonians 4:15 (CSB)**

*"But each in his own order: Christ, the firstfruits; afterward, **at his coming**, those who belong to Christ."* **1st Corinthians 15:23 (CSB)**

*"For who is our hope or joy or crown of boasting in the presence of our **Lord Jesus at his coming**? Is it not you?"* **1st Thessalonians 2:19 (CSB)**

*"So now, little children, remain in him so that when he appears we may have confidence and not be ashamed **before him at his coming**."* **1st John 2:28 (CSB)**

*"and then the lawless one will be revealed. The Lord Jesus will destroy him with the breath of his mouth and will bring him to nothing **at the appearance of his coming**."* **2nd Thessalonians 2:8 (CSB)**

After reading those verses, above, in context, it is obvious that there is only one **imminent** return of Christ. Another noteworthy point to highlight is that **1st Thessalonians 4:15** is not a **rapture** verse, but a **resurrection** verse which happens at **His second coming**.

CHAPTER TEN

MISHANDLING 1ST THESSALONIANS 4:13-17:

This is the biggest stumbling block for pre-tribulation adherents. The one place where all the scholars have let the Church down as a whole. By standing by and continuously misreading and misquoting this chapter they have allowed Satan to slip in and give the Church a false sense of hope that GOD ALMIGHTY has never confirmed through any single writer in the Old or New Testament. The Church has been warned by God to watch out for the doctrine of demons and the cunning craftiness of men who pervert the Word of God.

Let's examine this passage from Tim Lahaye and put his teachings under examination. Can it be supported by the Word Of GOD?

(bullet points are added to emphasized errors that has been presented as truth)

> "The Bible is clear: the coming of Christ for His church will be selective.
> * *The Rapture is not for everyone.*
> * *Only certain people will be included.*
> * *Some will be taken and others left.*
> * Two of the primary passages on the Rapture call them "those who are Christ's at His coming" (1 Corinthians 15:23) and "Those who sleep in Jesus" (or "the dead in Christ," 1 Thessalonians 4.14. 16).
> * The Rapture is for believers only (see 1 Thessalonians 4:14, 17).
> The clarification 'if we believe that Jesus died and rose again" clearly refers to those who have accepted the gospel "that Christ died for our sins according to the Scriptures, and that He was buried, and that He rose again the third day' (I Corinthians 15:3-4).
> * *Christ is not coming for the churches, implying church members, or merely for good people.*
> He will rapture only those who are in Him through believing on Him, receiving Him as their Lord and Savior."[34]

Take a closer look at **1st Thessalonians 4:13-17** line by line, contextually. Consistently, notice the subject matter of each line as it leads to the next.

> *"We do not want you to be **uninformed**, brothers and sisters, **concerning those who are asleep**, so that you will not grieve like the rest, **who have no hope.**"* **1st Thessalonians 4:13** (CSB)

The verse ensures us of our hope and informs us about the dead, so that we may be comforted and not grieve like the

---

34 Tim LaHaye, Rapture, Mubtnomah Publishers, 1998, p45

rest. So then what is the object of our hope? **Christ** and the **resurrection**.

> *"For **if we believe** that Jesus **died** and **rose again**, in **the same way**, through Jesus, God will bring with him **those who have fallen asleep.**"* 1ˢᵀ **THESSALONIANS 4:14 (CSB)**

Through our belief in Jesus, God will **resurrect** the **dead** the **same way** He did JESUS, through our belief in Jesus, we will be brought forth at **the resurrection**. The facts of Christ's experience are repeated in the believers. He died and then rose; so, believers shall die and then rise with Him.

The word '**with'** in verse 14 does not mean 'standing by His side'.

> G-4862 syn A primary preposition denoting union. This union arises from the addition or accession of one thing to another.

Christ first then us afterwards. Now let us back this up with Scripture:

> *"But each in his **own order: Christ**, the first fruits; **afterward**, at **his coming**, those who **belong to Christ**."* 1ˢᵀ **CORINTHIANS 15:23 (CSB)**

Notice *at his coming,* contextually it is referring to His Second Advent not at a pre-tribulation rapture of the Church, and the premise of the pre-tribulation is not supported by the text.

The text is consistent with a resurrection of the dead. The following verses time stamp and verify when this happens.

Here is what was said of **Jesus** and **Martha** about the **resurrection**.

> "'When Jesus arrived, he found that Lazarus had already been in the tomb four days. 18 Bethany was near Jerusalem (less than two miles away). 19 Many of the Jews had come to Martha and Mary to comfort them about their brother. 20 As soon as Martha heard that Jesus was coming, she went to meet him, but Mary remained seated in the house. 21 **Then Martha said to Jesus**, "Lord, if you had been here, my brother **wouldn't have died**. 22 Yet even now I know that whatever you ask from God, God will give you." 23
> - "**Your brother will rise again**," Jesus told her. 24
>   - Martha said to him, "I **know that he will rise again in the resurrection at the last day**." 25

- Jesus said to her, "I am the **resurrection** and the life. **The one who believes in me, even if he dies**, will live. 26 Everyone who lives and believes in me **will never die**. Do you believe this?" 27
  - "Yes, Lord," she told him, "I believe you are the Messiah, the Son of God, who comes into the world." **John 11: 17-27 (CSB)**

*"This is the **will of him** who **sent me**: that I should **lose none** of those he has given me but*
- ***should raise*** *them up on* ***the last day.****
*For this is the **will of my Father:** that everyone who sees the **Son** and **believes in him** will have **eternal life**,*
- *and I will **raise him up on the last day.****" **John 6: 39-40 (CSB)**

"For we say this to you by a word from the Lord: ***We who are still alive at the Lord's coming*** *will certainly **not precede** those who **have fallen asleep**." ****1ST** THESSALONIANS 4:15 (CSB)**

Are you getting the biblical message? The text clearly informs the Church that those who are alive and make it through to the end of the age (Christ second coming) will **not precede** or **go up to heaven before the dead**.

Friends, this is a problem. You might ask why is this an issue?

If the Word of God says, *the living will not go up before the dead* and in **Revelation chapter 20** there is a resurrection of the dead:

*"Then I saw thrones, and people seated on them who were given authority to judge. **I also saw the souls of those who had been beheaded** because of their testimony about Jesus and because of the word of God, who had not worshiped the beast or his image, and who had not accepted the mark on their foreheads or their hands. **They came to life and reigned with Christ for a thousand years**." **Revelation 20:4 (CSB)***

And in the verse 20:5 we are told *this is the first resurrection*; How then can anyone teach that the Church is going to go up before the dead are resurrected?

The dead who are resurrected are going to enter the Millennium Kingdom which will be in the holy city the same as those who came out of the ground:

> *"and the graves were opened; and **many bodies of the saints who had fallen asleep were raised;** 53 and coming out of the graves after His resurrection, **they went into the holy city and appeared to many.**"* **Matthew 27:52-53 (NKJV)**

The verse, **1st THESSALONIANS 4:15**, is noticeably clear! We who are alive and remain will **NOT PRECEDE the dead**.

The next logical question to ask the scholars who promote the pre-tribulation rapture, should be to show us evidence of a massive resurrection **before** the second coming of Christ!

HOW DO WE CLEAR THIS MISHANDLING UP?

> *"For the Lord himself will **descend from heaven** with a shout, with the archangel's voice, and with the trumpet of God, **and the dead in Christ will rise first**."* **1ST THESSALONIANS 4:16 (CSB)**

Once again, the verse says the Lord **will descend**, G-2597 katabaino[35] to come down from heaven.

Outline of Biblical Usage G-2597:
I. to go down, come down, descend
    A. the place from which one has come down from
    B. to come down
        i. as from the temple at Jerusalem, from the city of Jerusalem
        ii. of celestial beings coming down to earth

Did Christ stop in the **first heaven** or did he come **down to the** earth as the Scripture said?
Which line in the passage indicates a stop in the clouds, or is that a **doctrine of demons** added to give you a false hope in something that the Word of God has not said?

Notice also that verse 16 supports verse 15: It informs us that the resurrection must ~Will happen first. We can in total confidence of the Scripture conclude there is no mass resurrection before the second coming at the end of the age.

Here are a few examples of katabaino usage in Scripture:
- *"For I have **come down from heaven,** not to do My own will, but the will of Him who sent Me."* **John 6:38 (NKJV)**

- *"This is the bread which **comes down from heaven**, that one may eat of it and not die."* **John 6:50 (NKJV)**
- *"Then I saw an angel **coming down from heaven**, having the key to the bottomless pit and a great chain in his hand."* **Revelation 20:1 (NKJV)**
- *"Then I, John, saw the holy city, New Jerusalem, **coming down out of heaven** from God, prepared as a bride adorned for her husband."* Revelation 21:2 (NKJV)

Furthermore, verse 16 says the dead in Christ will rise first.

What kind of rise is the text referring to?

G-450 anistemi[36]:

Outline of Biblical Usage G-450:
  I. to cause to rise up, raise up
      A. raise up from laying down
      B. to raise up from the dead
      C. to raise up, cause to be born, to cause to appear, bring forward

This rise is to cause one to rise from laying down (or being raised from the dead) and not to catch one away in the sky.

Here are four examples of this word used in the same context:

- **Mark 9:9** *"as they were coming down the mountain, he ordered them to tell no one what they had seen until the Son of Man **had risen from the dead**."*
- **Luke 11:32** *"The men of Nineveh **will stand up** at the judgment with this generation and condemn it, because they repented at Jonah's preaching, and look -- something greater than Jonah is here."*
- **Luke 18:33** *"and after they flog him, they will kill him, and he will **rise on the third day**."*
- **John 11:23** *"your brother **will rise again**," Jesus told her.*

It is referring to the rise (*anistemi*) as in the **resurrection of the dead.** It is not referring to a rising in the sky. If so, we ask that the pre-tribulation scholars demonstrate that it is about the sky contextually without going to verse 17. Men have Interjected a **false narrative** that the text does not support.

---

[36] https://www.blueletterbible.org/lang/lexicon/lexicon.cfm?Strongs=G450&t=KJV

Saying that we meet the Lord in the sky is not supported by the text and gives a false view of Christ returning in the clouds, and not a single verse in Scripture supports this false premise. If so, please provide the book, chapter, and verse.

Here is the evidence that the scholars have missed; Verses 16 and 17 are separated by one thousand years *(a gap).*

(Notice, the quotes in this verse were added to highlight points that will be made.)

> *"'**Then**' we who are still alive, **who are left**, will be '**caught up**' '**together**', with them in the clouds to meet the Lord in the air, **and so we will always be with the Lord**."* **1ˢᵗ Thessalonians 4:17 (CSB)**

First, understand in verse 17 that the word '**then**', does not mean **immediately with**:

> G-1899 **epeita**[37] this word is used in *enumerations* which is the action of mentioning things ***one by one***. One thing then the other; also, of a time an order of things.

Outline of Biblical Usage G-1899
  I.   thereupon, thereafter, then, afterwards

Just as the verses have been showing us or laying it out for us.

> **First** the **resurrection**
> then or **afterward**
>   the **rapture**,

"*But each one in his own order: Christ the firstfruits, **afterward** those who are Christ's at His coming.*" **1 Corinthians 15:23 (NKJV)**

Notice three examples that confirm from the Blue Letter Bible that the word '***then***" in 1 Thessalonians 4:17 in context means 'afterward' or 'after that':

- 1 Co 15:7: ***After that,*** '*ᴳ¹⁸⁹⁹. he was seen of James; then of all the apostles.*
- 1 Co 15:23: *But every man in his own order: Christ the firstfruits;* ***afterward*** '*ᴳ¹⁸⁹⁹ they that are Christ's at his coming.*
- Gal 1:18: ***Then*** ᴳ¹⁸⁹⁹ *after three years I went up to Jerusalem to see Peter, and abode with him fifteen days.*[38]

---

[37] https://www.blueletterbible.org/lang/lexicon/lexicon.cfm?Strongs=G1899&t=KJV
[38] https://www.blueletterbible.org/lang/lexicon/lexicon.cfm?Strongs=G1899&t=KJV

Second, the word "***caught-up***" in 1ˢᵗ Thessalonians 4:17 in context means **both groups** are *caught up* <u>at the same time</u> and **NOT** *one* and **then** *the other*.

G-726 Harpazo ἁρπάζω harpázō, har-pad'-zo; from a derivative of G138; to seize (in various applications):—catch (away, up), pluck, pull, take (by force).[39]
Here are four examples:

> - **John 6:15 (CSB)** *Therefore, when Jesus realized that they were about to come **and take him by force** to make him king, he withdrew again to the mountain by himself.*
> - **Acts 8:39 (CSB)** *When they came up out of the water, the Spirit of the Lord **carried Philip away**, and the eunuch did not see him any longer but went on his way rejoicing.*
> - **2 Corinthians 12:2 (CSB)** *I know a man in Christ **who was caught up** to the third heaven fourteen years ago. Whether he was in the body or out of the body, I don't know; God knows.*
> - **Revelation 12:5 (CSB)** *She gave birth to a Son, a male who is going to rule all nations with an iron rod. Her child **was caught up** to God and to his throne.*

Third, the Greek word (Harpazo) in 1ˢᵗ Thessalonians 4:17 means *to be caught up, or snatched away, or taken by force*. Also, in verse 16, we are informed that the dead that were just resurrected and those who live and remain, **happens after the resurrection, NOT** at the same time. Why do I call your attention to this point? The next word we explain will give more clarity as to why the pre-trib position is not supported by the Greek language.

G-260 Hama, ἅμα háma, ham'-ah; a primary particle; properly, **at the "same" time**, but freely used as a preposition or adverb denoting close association:—also, and, **together**, with(-al).[40]

Here are a few examples:
1 Thessalonians 4:17 Then we which are alive and remain shall be caught up together 'G260' with them in the clouds, to meet the Lord in the air: and so shall we ever be with the Lord.
- Mat 13:29 *But he said, Nay; lest while ye gather up the tares, ye root up also the wheat **with** 'G260' **them**".*

---

[39] https://www.blueletterbible.org/lang/lexicon/lexicon.cfm?Strongs=G726&t=KJV
[40] https://www.blueletterbible.org/lang/lexicon/lexicon.cfm?Strongs=G260&t=KJV

- *Mat 20:1   For the kingdom of heaven is like unto a man that is an householder, which went out early in the morning 'G260' **to hire labourers** into his vineyard.*
- *Rom 3:12 They are all gone out of the way, **they are together** 'G260' become unprofitable; there is none that doeth good, no, not one.*
- *Col 4:3 Withal 'G260' **praying also for us**, that God would open unto us a door of utterance, to speak the mystery of Christ, for which I am also in bonds:*

Fourth, the Greek word *Hama* (together) is used in such a way that both groups:

- **the resurrected** and
- **those who** are alive and remain

must be snatched away at the same time. This means the Pretribulationist' premise is not supported by the text. Their view teaches that **the dead rise** in the clouds **then** *the living* follows after them.

The word (Hama) in the Greek shows that <u>both groups</u> would **go up or be caught up at the exact same time** (together). Hama does **NOT** mean or imply:

- That the resurrected group would be caught up
- then
  - those who were alive would immediately follow them, afterward.

This is what the Pre-tribulation view teaches. Now let's not forget to examine the space in between verses 16 and 17 in 1st Thessalonians chapter 4. I am aware that people will say and ask, '**What!!! Show me that in Scripture**' (smile); I am glad you want me to prove this.

CHAPTER ELEVEN

THE RESURRECTION PRECEDES THE RAPTURE

In the last chapter I made a claim, and therefore, I bear the burden of proof; and through the aid of Scripture, I will do just that, prove it!

As good Bible students it is our job to study to show ourselves approved before God and to go to the farthest lengths to prove exactly what God has written and would have the Church to exegete, being of one mind in our learning. The truth is that there is only one Biblical Truth, in Christ Jesus.

As we precede, it is imperative that we are willing to patiently investigate the **long-form evidence** that overwhelmingly proves that the second advent resurrection that Jesus spoke of comes before the rapture.

Too often information provided by Paul is overlooked. He wrote in 1st Corinthians 15:3-49 is consistently about the resurrection.

- He reminds the Thessalonians about the resurrection of the dead. (**1 Thessalonians 4:13-16**)
  - He encourages the Thessalonians in the knowledge they had already received about the resurrection.
    - We know this by the way the letter continues:
      *"About the times and the seasons: Brothers and sisters, **you do not need anything to be written** to you. 2 For **you yourselves know very well** that the day of the Lord will come just like a thief in the night."* **1 Thessalonians 5:1-2 (CSB)**
- Furthermore, Paul in 1st Corinthians 15:50-58 gives you the long-form of what is written in 1st Thessalonians 4:17 information about the rapture.

The shift from **the Resurrection** to **the Rapture** happens in verses 49 and 50 of 1st Corinthians chapter 15. In the same fashion, Paul does the same shift in 1st Thessalonians chapter 4 between verses 16 and 17. Consequently, what we have received from Paul and his writings is the long-form and short form of the same message with fewer details.

The Resurrection. For more details on 1 Corinthians 15 review

1ST CORINTHIANS 15:42-49:

42 *"So it is with the **resurrection of the dead**:*
- *Sown in corruption, **raised in incorruption**;*
- *sown in dishonor, **raised in glory**;*
- *sown in weakness, **raised in power**;*
- *sown a natural body, **raised a spiritual body**. If there is a natural body, **there is also a spiritual body**.*
- *49 And just as we have borne the image of the man of dust, **we will also bear the image of the man of heaven**.*

In this chapter the **resurrection** is pronounced first, as the chapter continues, we see the mention of the **rapture** and it specifically tells us **the bodies will be changed to be raptured**.

1ST CORINTHIANS 15:50-55:

- "50 What I am saying, brothers and sisters, is this: **Flesh** and **blood cannot inherit the kingdom of God**, nor can corruption inherit incorruption. 51 **Listen**, I **am telling you** a **mystery**:
  - **We will not all fall asleep**,
  - but we will all **be changed**,
- 52 in a **moment**, in **the twinkling of an eye**, at **the last trumpet**. For the trumpet will sound,
  - and the **dead will be raised incorruptible**,
  - and **we will be changed**.
- 53 For this **corruptible body must be clothed with incorruptibility**, and this **mortal body must be clothed with immortality**."

Notice in verses 52-53: There is a change to those that were raised from the dead, and there is also the change of those who are alive and still have corruptible bodies from what the text says. These two groups are raptured at the end of the Millennium together.

This event happens in the twinkle of an eye at the last trumpet. Both groups get a glorified body at this point; The dead who died during the Millennium and those who lived through it.

But Scripture demonstrates that both events are separated by a thousand years.

THE RAPTURED

Verse 54 "**When** this corruptible body **is clothed** with **incorruptibility**, and this mortal body is **clothed with immortality**,

- **then** the saying that is **written will take place**:
  - Death has been **swallowed** up in **victory**. Where, **death**, is **your victory**? Where, death, is **your sting**?"

Reading the verses in context proves the **resurrection precedes** the **rapture.** What may confuse most people is that there is more than one resurrection (all considered the First Resurrection), but there is absolutely only one rapture.

The first mass resurrection happens at the LORD'S return, and the second one happens at the end of the Millennium as the Scripture has prescribed. Hence, there is a thousand-year separation.

We can conclude that our statement is true, *the resurrection precedes* the rapture, because in 1st Thessalonians 4:16-17 these two verses are separated by 1000 years:

- *"16 **For the Lord himself will descend from heaven with a shout,** with the archangel's voice, and with the trumpet of God, **and the dead in Christ will rise first.***

- *17 **Then we who are still alive, who are left, will be caught up together with them** in the clouds to meet the Lord in the air, and so we will always be with the Lord."*

__1000YEAR SEPARATION:__

> **1ST CORINTHIANS 15:20-23** "But as it is, Christ has been **raised** from the dead, the **firstfruits** of those who have **fallen asleep**. 21 For since death came through a man, **the resurrection** of the **dead** also comes through a man. 22For just as in Adam all die, **so also in Christ all will be made alive**. 23 But each **in his own order**: Christ, the firstfruits; afterward, **at his coming**, those who **belong to Christ**.

In the above verses, we see the Resurrection expressed out at His coming, and the next three verse are 1000 years away. The **Resurrection** happens at the beginning of the Millennium so **when does verses 24 -26 happen**?

> *1st Corinthians 15:24-26 Then comes **the end**, when he **hands over the kingdom** to God the Father, when **he abolishes all rule** and all authority **and power**. For he must **reign** until he puts **all his enemies under his feet**. The **last enemy** to be abolished is death.*

When does the Bible say that Christ shall **hand over** all rule and put an end to **death**?

> "Then I heard a loud voice from the throne: Look,
> - **God's dwelling is with humanity, and he will live with them**. They will be his peoples, and God himself will be with them and will be their God. 4
> - **He will wipe away every tear from their eyes**.
>   - **Death will be no more**;
>   - grief, crying, and pain will be no more, because the **previous things** have passed away. 5
> - **Then the one seated on the throne said, "Look, I am making everything new." 6**
>   - He also said, "Write, because these words are faithful and true."
> - Then he said to me, "**It is done!** I am the Alpha and the Omega, the beginning and the end. I will freely give to the thirsty from the spring of the **water of life**. 7 The one who **conquers** will **inherit these things**, and I will be his God, and he will be my son." **Revelation 21:3-7 (CSB)**

Now we know that the verses point to the end of the Millennium when Christ puts an end to death and **completes all things**.

Lining up the Scriptures from the Old and New Testament to understand scripturally the verses separated by 1000 years.

The following verses are given to support our premise that

- • *information* given in Scripture can be close together in the written text (same verse, paragraph, etc.),
- • but *the events* in that *information* can be separated by years.

> *"On this mountain, the Lord of Armies will prepare for all the peoples a feast of choice meat, a feast with aged wine, prime cuts of choice meat, fine vintage wine. 7 On this mountain he will destroy the burial shroud, the shroud over all the peoples, the sheet covering all the nations; 8 he will destroy death forever. The Lord God will wipe away the tears from every face and remove his people's disgrace from the whole earth, for the Lord has spoken."* **Isaiah 25:6-8 (CSB)**

Isaiah 25: 6 is a reference to the thousand-year reign of Christ when he returns.

> *"'Again, he sent out other servants and said, 'Tell those who are invited: See, I've prepared my dinner; my oxen and fattened cattle have been slaughtered, and everything is ready. Come to the wedding banquet. '"* **Matthew 22:4 (CSB)**

Scripture backs that up:

> *"For I tell you, from now on I will not drink of the fruit of the vine until the kingdom of God comes."* **Luke 22:18 (CSB)**

From our study, we know that these things did not take place in the Lord's first advent. This sets the timeframe for this verse at the Millennium when the Kingdom comes to earth.

Now **Isaiah 25:7-8** expresses how Christ ends all death in the world.
- • The **shroud** is the **death shroud** that covers the dead.
- • There is also a reference to **wiping away every tear**.

When does this happen? It happens at **the end of the Millennium** and at the **beginning of Eternity**.

Now as we see these things expressed in the verses, the biblical picture starts to form in our minds. The marriage super of the Lamb and the end of all things being put Under Christ feet are separated by 1000 years also.

WHERE SHOULD WE LOOK TO VERILY THIS?

> *"Then I saw a new heaven and a new earth;*
> - *• for the first heaven and the first earth had passed away, and the sea was no more. 2*

- *I also **saw the holy city, the new Jerusalem, coming down out** of **heaven** from God, **prepared like** a bride adorned for her husband. 3*
- *Then I heard a loud voice from the throne: Look, God's dwelling is with humanity, and he will live with them. They will be his peoples, and God himself will be with them and will be their God.*
  - *4 **He will wipe away every tear from their eyes.***
  - ***Death will be no more**; grief, crying, and pain will be no more,*

  because the previous things have passed away."
  REVELATION 21:1-4 (CSB)

John 5:28-29 paint a simple picture but are also events separated by **1000 years**.

> "Do not be amazed at this, because a **time** is **coming** when all who **are in the graves** will hear his voice 29 and **come out** —
> - those who have **done good** things, to the **resurrection of life**,
> - but those who have **done wicked** things, to the **resurrection** of **condemnation**." John 5:28-29 (CSB)

How do we understand the separation in verse **29 of** the **resurrection** of **life**, and the **resurrection** of **condemnation**? **Where do we go?**

Resurrection of Life:
> "Then I saw thrones, and people seated on them who were given authority to judge.
> - I also **saw the souls of those who had been beheaded because of their testimony** about **Jesus** and because of the **word of God**,
>   - who had **not worshiped the beast** or his image,
>   - and who **had not accepted the mark** on their foreheads or their hands.
> - **They came to life and reigned with**
>   - **Christ for** a **thousand years.** 5
>   - The **rest of the dead** did not come to life
>   - **until the thousand years** were completed.
>   - **This is the first resurrection. Revelation 20:4-5**

The Resurrection of Condemnation:
> "Then I saw a **great white throne** and one seated on it. Earth and heaven fled from his presence, **and no place was found for them.** 12

- *I also saw **the dead**, the great and the small, standing before the throne, and books were opened. Another book was opened, which is the book of life,*
- **and the dead were judged according to their works** *by what was* **written in the books.** *13*
  - *Then the sea gave up the dead that were in it,* **and death** *and* **Hades** *gave* **up the dead** *that were in them;*
  - **each one was judged according to their works.** *14*
  - *Death and Hades were thrown into the lake of fire.*

This is the second death, the lake of fire. *15*

- *And anyone whose name* **was not found written** *in the book of life was* **thrown** *into the* **lake of fire.*** **Revelation 20:11-15 (CSB)**

The evidence from the Word of God is overwhelming. The truth and evidence have been properly presented allowing Scripture to verify Scripture. Not only does the Resurrection precede the Rapture, but also, we see in 1st Thessalonians 4:16-17 that there is a thousand-year gap.

CHAPTER TWELVE

WHEN DOES THE RAPTURE HAPPEN?

In this chapter, the main issue of this book is addressed, when does the rapture happen?

There have been many different views on the subject of when does the rapture happen; or how many times does Christ returns to the earth or in the air; and what are the phases.

At this point, rational reasoning should prevail; both the writings of Paul and the teachings of Jesus are clear, precise, and compelling.

It is sufficed to say, this book does not hold to any of these views:
- Pre-tribulation view
- Mid tribulation view
- Post-tribulation view

It holds and affirms the Biblical view.

These last verses that we will examine focuses on what Jesus revealed to Paul. Are you prepared to be obedient to the Word of God as prescribed to the letter? The believers in Jesus Christ, who make it their practice to study the Word of God, understands it is our job to deeply search-out the truth in context of All Scripture. Our Lord and Savior Jesus Christ has raised us up as Biblical Soldiers; our purpose is to prove and protect our brothers and sisters from error both foreign and domestic.

We are to be as bold as the Lord would lead us to be. Our job is to seek truth and not to weigh the words of a man based on his titles or labels associated with his name. We serve the true and living God. *"prove all things; hold fast that which is good."* **1st Thessalonians 5:21 (KJV)**

WHEN DOES THE BIBLE SAY THE RAPTURE HAPPENS?

The evidence has already been given to us; you be the judge.

Connecting the Biblical dots (verses):

Connecting the verses together paints the full picture.

Reading in context, line by line, and verse by verse with the full view of Scripture in mind; **Finally, let us finish this up.**

THE RESURRECTION OF THE DEAD COMES FIRST:

> ### 1 Corinthians Chapter 15:
> *"20 But as it is, Christ has been raised from the dead, the firstfruits of those **who have fallen asleep**. 21 For since*
> - **death** *came through* **a man,**
> - **the resurrection of the dead** *also comes through* **a man.**
>
> *22 For just as in Adam all die, so also in Christ all will be made alive. 23 But* **each in his own order: Christ, the firstfruits;**
> - **afterward, at his coming, those** *who belong to Christ.*

Notice in verses 21 through 23, it is clear Paul is teaching the order of the Resurrection and expressing that through Adam all men would die, but that all who are in Christ will be resurrected at His Second Coming.

> - **24 Then** *comes the end,*
>   - *when* **he hands over** *the kingdom* **to God the Father,**
>   - *when he abolishes all rule and all authority and power.*
> *25* ***For he must reign until***
> - ***he puts all his enemies under his feet****. 26*
>   - *The* **last enemy** *to be abolished is* **death.**
> *27 For God has put everything under his feet.*
> ***Now when it says "everything" is put under him,***
> - *it is obvious that he who puts everything under him is the exception. 28*
> - *When everything is subject to Christ,*
>   - **then** *the Son himself will also be subject to the one who subjected everything to him, so that God may be all in all.)*

In Verses 24 through 28, Paul has given us an immediate (telescopic prophecy) of what happens at the end of the Millennium period, which would be a thousand years from the Resurrection when Christ returns at His Second Advent.

Here are the details:
1) He hands over the Kingdom to God the Father,
2) and abolishes or puts an end to all rule and authority, which is expressed out in detail in Revelation 21:4-6;
   a. when death is put under His feet
   b. and all is completed with the last of all prophetic literature.

> *29 Otherwise what will they do who are being baptized for the dead? If the dead are not raised at all, then why are people baptized for them? 30 Why are we in danger every hour? 31 I face death every day, as surely as I may boast about you, brothers and sisters, in Christ Jesus our Lord. 32 If I fought wild beasts in Ephesus as a mere man, what good did that do me?* **If the dead are not raised**, *Let us eat and drink, for* **tomorrow we die**. *33 Do not be deceived: "Bad company corrupts good morals." 34 Come to your senses and stop sinning; for some people are ignorant about God. I say this to your shame. 35 But someone will ask, "How are the dead raised?*

At this point in verses 29 through 35, Paul is still teaching about the resurrection and defending against proxy baptism's which is the belief that those who are alive can be baptized for those who have died already. This is a false teaching that Paul was defending against.

> ***"What kind of body will they have when they come?"***
> *36*
> - ***You fool!*** *What you sow does not come to life unless it dies. 37*
> - *And as for what you sow — you are not sowing the body that will be, but only a seed, perhaps of wheat or another grain. 38*
> - **But God** *gives it a body as he wants, and to each of the seeds its own body.*
> *39 Not all flesh is the same flesh; there is one flesh for humans, another for animals, another for birds, and another for fish. 40 There are* **heavenly bodies** *and* **earthly bodies,**
> - *but the splendor of* **the heavenly bodies** *is different from that of* **the earthly ones**. *41 There is a splendor of the sun, another of the moon, and another of the stars; in fact, one star differs from another star in splendor. 42*
> - ***So it is with the resurrection of the dead:***

- o *Sown in corruption, raised in incorruption; 43 sown in dishonor, raised in glory;*
- o *sown in weakness, raised in power; 44*
- o *sown a natural body, raised a spiritual body.*

If there is a natural body, there is also a spiritual body. 45 So it is written, The first man Adam became a living being; the last Adam became a life-giving spirit. 46 However, the spiritual is not first, but the natural, then the spiritual.

47 The first man was from the earth, a man of dust; the second man is from heaven. 48 Like the man of dust, so are those who are of the dust; like the man of heaven, so are those who are of heaven. 49 And just as we have borne the image of the man of dust, we will also bear the image of the man of heaven.

Paul explains, in verses 36-49, the differences between the two natures of mankind:

1) The *fallen State* which we received from Adam
2) And the *New Birth* which we receive in Christ.

The core word in the passage above is image (v49).

G-1504[41] eikon Image

Outline of Biblical Usage

I.   an image, figure, likeness
   A.   an image of the things (the heavenly things)
      i.   used of the moral likeness of renewed men to God
      ii.   the image of the Son of God, **into which true Christians are transformed**, is likeness not only to the heavenly body, but also to the most holy and blessed state of mind, which Christ possesses

Paul is conveying in the message how that believers must bear this same image before entering into the Kingdom of God.

Here are three examples of how the word "eikon" is used in the context:

- ➤ **Romans 8:29 (CSB)** *For those he foreknew he also predestined to be conformed **to the image of his Son**, so that he would be the firstborn among many brothers and sisters.*
- ➤ **2 Corinthians 3:18 (CSB)** *We all, with unveiled faces, are looking as in a mirror at the glory of the Lord and are **being transformed into the same image** from glory to glory; this is from the Lord who is the Spirit.*
- ➤ **Colossians 3:10 (CSB)** *and have put on the new self. You are being renewed in knowledge according to **the image of your Creator**.*

---

[41] https://www.blueletterbible.org/lang/lexicon/lexicon.cfm?Strongs=G1504&t=KJV

> 50 *"**What I am saying**, brothers and sisters, **is this:***
> - ***Flesh and blood cannot inherit the kingdom of God**, nor can corruption inherit incorruption."*

In verse 50, Paul explains that the flesh (G4561-sarx) or the sensuous nature of man cannot enter heaven.

G4561 [42] -sarx - Flesh
Outline of Biblical Usage
C. the sensuous nature of man, "the animal nature"

   i.   without any suggestion of depravity
   ii.   the animal nature with cravings which incite to sin
   iii.   the physical nature of man as subject to suffering

As we follow the text, Paul is expressing that this nature found in man will not be translated up to the presence of God. This is also expressed above in verses 36-49. Here are four examples of the word "*sarx* or flesh" being used in context: **Matthew 26:41, John 3:6, Romans 7:18, 1st Corinthians 1:26.**

> - *51 Listen, I am telling you a mystery:*
>   - ○ *We will not all fall asleep,*
>   - ○ *but we will all be changed,*

Paul expounds expressing what the mystery is and provides all the details (the Shew) to the mystery about this *change* in verses 51- 54.

G-3004 [43] ~ lego ~ shew - telling
Outline of Biblical Usage [?]
   I.   to say, to speak
      A. affirm over, maintain
      B. to teach
      C. to exhort, advise, to command, direct
      D. to point out with words, intend, mean, mean to say
      E. to call by name, to call, name
      F. to speak out, speak of, mention

Too often, many people, stop at the evidence of the rapture and attempt to make only the Rapture the mystery. They say that the mystery was that "*there would be a Rapture*."

---

[42] https://www.blueletterbible.org/lang/lexicon/lexicon.cfm?Strongs=G4561&t=KJV

[43] https://www.blueletterbible.org/lang/lexicon/lexicon.cfm?Strongs=G3004&t=KJV

They stopped prematurely at that point. However, as we see in Scripture, Paul went further and explains more about the mystery, such as

- the time frame in great detail,
- and the prerequisites to things that must happen to the human body.

Through an understanding of eschatology, we know that these details point the Biblical reader to an exact reference in biblical prophecy.

- o *52 in a moment, in the twinkling of an eye, at the last trumpet. For the trumpet will sound, and the dead will be raised incorruptible,*
- *and we will be changed.*

Paul is now showing that the Rapture will suddenly take place at the **last** G2078-(eschatos) **trumpet.** This word "eschatos" is defined as the very last of a thing.

G2078 (eschatos) - last
Outline of Biblical Usage
I. extreme
    A. *last in time or in place*
    B. last in a series of places
    C. *last in a temporal succession*
II. the last
    A. **last, referring to time**
    B. **of space, the uttermost part, the end, of the earth**
    C. of rank, grade of worth, last i.e. lowest

The question is what are the series of things that must take place at the very last trumpet? Paul has given a view of biblical prophecy which is expressed in Revelation chapters 20:7 through 21:4 when Satan and the nations surround The Holy City and then Christ brings down fire from heaven.

After this event, John sees a New Heaven and New earth coming down from heaven.

The next question would be what happened between these events "*the war against the Holy city*" and "the New Heaven and New Earth" **in the blink of an eye?** The answer is *The Bride comes down from Heaven!*

Finally, how did **the bride** (The *Church*) get into heaven when she was just on the earth surround by Satan and the nations (**Revelation 20:7-10**)? The answer is **The Rapture**.

> *"53 For this corruptible body must be clothed with* ***incorruptibility***, *and this* ***mortal body*** *must be clothed with immortality. 54* ***When this corruptible body is clothed with incorruptibility***, *and* ***this mortal body is clothed with immortality***,*
> - ***then the saying that is written will take place: Death has been swallowed up in victory***. *55*
>   - *Where, death, is your victory? Where, death, is your sting? "* **1ˢᵗ Corinthians 15:20-55 (CSB)**

The million-dollar question is this, when does death get swallowed up in victory?

> *"'I heard a loud voice from the throne: Look, God's dwelling is with humanity, and he will live with them. They will be his peoples, and God himself will be with them and will be their God. 4* ***He will wipe away every tear from their eyes. Death will be no more;*** *grief, crying, and pain will be no more, because the previous things have passed away. 5 Then the one seated on the throne said, "****Look, I am making everything new.****" He also said, "Write, because these words are faithful and true." 6 Then he said to me, "****It is done!*** *I am the Alpha and the Omega, the beginning and the end. I will freely give to the thirsty from the spring of the water of life."'*
> **Revelation 21:3-6 (CBS)**

This brings us to the point that the Apostle Paul said in the scripture about **the body** has to put on **incorruptibility** and **immorality**, these two attributes must be given to the people **who live until the end of the Millennium**.

Why one may ask? If you recall that we observed in our studied:
1) in the Millennium men will still have **the sin nature** and cannot go into **the Eternal state** until they are **changed**.
2) Also, the **prerequisite** of the verse says, When this **corruptible body** has put on **incorruptibility** and this **mortal** has put on immortality, **then the saying that is written takes PLACE.**

Of course, the thing that was written was *DEATH WHERE IS YOUR STING OH DEATH WHERE IS YOUR VICTORY?*

So, the Biblical view in conclusion is that the **RAPTURE** does not take place until the end of the **MILLENNIUM** and the beginning of **ETERNITY!**

Take note! The apostle Paul is the writer of both books that mention the rapture and was the authority on the matter.

Congratulations "All Believers Make it!" Well family and friends, this has been fun. See you at the **RAPTURE.**

APPENDIX

ABOUT THE AUTHOR

Andrew Eugene Hooper has served as a minister and apologist for the last five years. He currently is a member of Strictly Biblical Bible Teaching Ministries.

He has debated many Hebrew Israelite Camp leaders and individuals on Bible Doctrine. He teaches weekly on Facebook expounding on Hermeneutic approaches of Biblical study; Christian Living and exposing false doctrines of various cultic groups. He is a continued student of the Bible and spends a considerable amount of time carrying the gospel of Jesus Christ to the streets weekly. The BUS-STOPS "is" his pulpit!

Previously served as an ironworker for local 25 for ten years building up metro Detroit and surrounding areas. Graduated from Mumford High School in 1992. I am currently dedicated to teaching the gospel, providing biblical counseling, and defending the faith.

About The Author

CPSIA information can be obtained
at www.ICGtesting.com
Printed in the USA
BVHW090957070222
628285BV00013B/483

9 780578 819730